Dr Peter Vardy has been Vice-Principal of Heythrop College, the specialist philosophy and theology college of the University of London, since 1999. He lectures internationally to teachers and students and is committed to providing a spiritual perspective in an increasingly secular and postmodern world. He is a best-selling author whose books include *The Puzzle of God*, *The Puzzle of Sex*, *The Puzzle of Ethics*, *Being Human* and, with Julie Arliss, *The Thinker's Guide to Evil* and *The Thinker's Guide to God*.

An Introduction to

Kierkegaard

Peter Vardy

 HENDRICKSON
PUBLISHERS

First published in Great Britain in 1996 as *Kierkegaard*
by Fount Paperbacks, an imprint of HarperCollins Publishers,
and in the United States in 1997 by Triumph Publishing.

This revised and expanded edition published jointly in 2008

as *The SPCK Introduction to Kierkegaard* by
Society for Promoting Christian Knowledge
36 Causton Street
London SW1P 4ST

and as *An Introduction to Kierkegaard* by
Hendrickson Publishers, Inc
P.O. Box 3473
Peabody, Massachusetts 01961-3473

Copyright © Peter Vardy 1996, 2008

British Library Cataloguing-in-Publication Data
A catalogue record for this book is available from the British Library

SPCK ISBN 978–0–281–05986–7
Hendrickson Publishers ISBN 978–1–59856–345–0

1 3 5 7 9 10 8 6 4 2

Typeset by Graphicraft Ltd, Hong Kong
Printed in Great Britain by Ashford Colour Press

Produced on paper from sustainable forests

This book is dedicated to
'that solitary individual'

Contents

Preface

For 25 years I have taught an undergraduate course in Kierkegaard at Heythrop College, the largely Jesuit-run specialist philosophy and theology college of the University of London. It is a very special place, combining the highest standards of academic rigour and open-mindedness with a clear faith orientation. Many students throughout the years have influenced me with their passion and interest in Kierkegaard and the connections they have made between Kierkegaard and many other philosophers, theologians and psychologists, but I am particularly grateful to Charlotte Fowler, Rob Hampson, John Handford and Felicity McCutcheon.

My mother, Christa Lund Vardy, was Danish and left me with a great admiration for all that this small country has achieved. She died in 1975 and one of my regrets is not to have been able to share with her something of what Kierkegaard has taught me. On a personal level he has influenced me more than any other thinker.

Dr Peter Vardy

Abbreviations

AC	*Attack upon Christendom*, tr. Walter Lowrie
CA	*The Concept of Anxiety*, tr. Reidar Thompte
CUP	*Concluding Unscientific Postscript*, tr. Walter Lowrie and David Swenson
ED	*Eighteen Edifying Discourses*, tr. Walter Lowrie (Oxford: Oxford University Press)
EO	*Either/Or*, tr. David and Lillian Swenson
FSE	*For Self-Examination*, tr. Walter Lowrie
FT	*Fear and Trembling*, tr. Alistair Hannay (Harmondsworth: Penguin)
J	*Journals*, tr. Howard and Edna Hong
PF	*Philosophical Fragments*, tr. David Swenson
PH	*Purity of Heart is to Will One Thing*, tr. Douglas Steere (New York: Harper Torchbooks)
SD	*The Sickness unto Death*, tr. Walter Lowrie
SLW	*Stages on Life's Way*, tr. Howard and Edna Hong
TC	*Training in Christianity*, tr. Walter Lowrie
WL	*Works of Love*, tr. Howard and Edna Hong

Except where indicated, all of the above editions are published by Princeton University Press.

Introduction

At one level, Kierkegaard's aim is straightforward: to strip you, the reader, naked at two in the morning, to sit you in front of a mirror and to force you to think about your life. His books are addressed to 'that solitary individual' who may be willing to listen to what he says and to ask questions about his or her own life. He demands a willingness for self-examination, which many usually seek to avoid; he demands a willingness to take off the masks which everyone wears in everyday life and to be ruthlessly honest about what is true and false. Kierkegaard considers that we are all prone to self-deceit and he gives us his readers no peace until we can see ourselves truthfully, as a prelude to making decisions about the manner in which we should live.

In J. K. Rowling's Harry Potter books, the young wizard Harry discovers the mirror of Erisaid. This is a remarkable magical mirror; those who stare into it will see nothing less than the deepest desires of their hearts. It does not necessarily reveal the future. It reveals what the person yearns for most and this desire may or may not be satisfied in the future. The mirror enables people to confront and to address their desires, to ask whether or not this is what they should desire or what they really want to desire, and it gives them an opportunity to change the direction of their lives. Professor Dumbledore, Harry Potter's inspiration and guide, says to him that those who look into the mirror and sees nothing else but themselves, just as they are, would have nothing more to desire and would be truly happy. Kierkegaard would have approved of the mirror as it would at least force you and I to engage with reality.

It might seem from this that Kierkegaard is a psychologist – and so he is, well before Freud or Jung. However, he is also a brilliant philosopher and Christian theologian. He brings the three disciplines together in a remarkable way. Yet, though he is a philosopher, theologian and psychologist, there is also a sense in which he would have rejected all these disciplines. This is because they can be used to objectify knowledge so that it ceases to relate to the individual. In their technicalities, cleverness and desire to develop a complete and coherent account of what it is to be human, they lose sight of the real experience of humanity and become 'untrue' and irrelevant in a sense. In all his writings he is passionately committed to communicate from heart to heart, to help 'his reader', that person who reads his works at a distance in time and place, to think deeply about his or her life and to make decisions about how to live – and how to die.

Kierkegaard has been described by many as 'the father of existentialism'. This is misleading. Existentialism was a twentieth-century movement particularly influenced by Jean-Paul Sartre which emphasized personal autonomy, individual freedom and the capacity for individual choice. In that Kierkegaard was concerned with the individual and with philosophy that related to life, the description of him as 'the father of existentialism' may be relevant, but for many existentialists, truth depends on the individual and Kierkegaard would have rejected this. Kierkegaard was a philosophical realist maintaining a correspondence theory of truth in the classical tradition; as such, his work can illuminate the debate between realism and non-realism in contemporary philosophy. His great philosophical opponent was Georg Wilhelm Friedrich Hegel (1770–1831). Hegel saw truth emerging through history as a result of the dialectical process. A view was put forward (a thesis) and this view met strong opposition from those who rejected it entirely and who put forward a totally opposed view (the antithesis). Initially these views appeared irreconcilable but, Hegel held, they became reconciled over time (the synthesis). As the new synthesis was accepted it became in effect a new thesis, which would provoke an antithesis . . . and so the process continued.

Hegel's philosophical nickname was 'Both/And' since he held that two seemingly contradictory statements can both be true. He was the forerunner of philosophies which claim that truth depends on the situation, that it is not absolute but relative. Kierkegaard saw himself, by contrast with Hegel, as 'Either/Or' – *either* statements are true *or* they are false, depending on whether or not they correspond to the state of affairs which they describe, not on how those affairs are perceived. This is a traditional realist position and one of great contemporary relevance.

Kierkegaard challenged and criticized the Christian milieu in which he lived, but he did not really address the issue of other world religions and their truth-claims. His work can and should be applied to the issue of contemporary inter-religious dialogue, however, and this book will attempt to do so.

Today, there is real interest in Kierkegaard's approach from a range of different countries and cultures. His philosophy is seen to have enduring and widespread relevance, but it is not a simple approach, it is not possible to say, 'Read this book by Kierkegaard and you will be clear about his argument'. His many books and articles are written from multitudes of perspectives, often under pseudonyms and sometimes under layers of pseudonyms. He makes considerable demands on the reader just because his message is that the search for truth and meaning demands personal engagement and struggle. There are no easy answers, so Kierkegaard does not try to package his teachings to make them accessible and palatable. The greatest demand is that the reader should have an interest in his or her own life and how it is lived. This, for Kierkegaard, is the starting point of good philosophy. The word 'philosophy' means 'love of wisdom' and wisdom can only be gained through experience and reflection. Any so-called philosophy which does not engage the individual, reflect the life they have experienced and affect the life they go on to live is no more than tiddly-winks – a game that may pass the time but is of no more significance than that. He was critical of much of the philosophy of his time, and would have been even more critical of much contemporary philosophy, as it failed to engage with real life. He looked back to the model of the great Greek philosophers, who saw philosophy as an essentially practical discipline – the sorting and drawing together of experience to provide truths about how life should be lived, how countries should be governed, issues of Justice, Truth and the Good Life. For Kierkegaard, philosophy should not be an abstract discipline but should be grounded in what it is to be human, and it should have relevance to all aspects of our existence. He wrote, 'I also know that in Greece a thinker was not a stunted existing person who produced works of art, but he himself was an existing work of art' (CUP 303).

Kierkegaard had an abiding interest in the nature of love between human beings, although he forces his reader to go beyond superficial categories. If you say to someone, 'I love you', Kierkegaard would want you to ask yourself precisely what you mean by these words. He does not think the issue is at all clear. The same applies, but on a deeper and more profound level, with the question 'What does it mean to be a self?' Kierkegaard argues that the answer is far from obvious and, indeed, he maintains that most people are not selves at all. Being a self, being an individual, is challenging and it is something that few attempt. Instead we 'construct ourselves' so that we are acceptable to others – we become a copy; we put on a mask. Truly being a self is too hard and one of Kierkegaard's main aims in forcing us to look at ourselves is to ask ourselves who we are:

> The biggest danger, that of losing oneself, can pass off in the world as quietly as if it were nothing; every other loss, an arm, a leg, five dollars, a wife, etc. is bound to be noticed. (CUP 62–3)

In other words, most of us forget who we are – we become so focused on creating a mask that is pleasing and acceptable to our peers, our colleagues, our parents, our partners that, beneath the mask, we never realize that 'I' as an individual has ceased to exist:

> They use their abilities, amass wealth, carry out worldly enter-prises, make prudent calculations, etc. and perhaps are men-tioned in history, but they are not themselves. In a spiritual sense they have no self, no self for whose sake they could venture everything. (CUP 64–5)

The lack of being an individual, our failure to be a self, leads to despair – a fact which most of us may never acknowledge. We convince ourselves that life is 'happy', that there is meaning and pur-pose to our lives, when often this is not the case. We throw ourselves into activity of various kinds which is subconsciously designed to prevent us having to think deeply about ourselves at all. However, instead of considering despair as negative, Kierkegaard actually believes that the pain of despair can help us to recognize our situ-ation. Thus despair is positive as it can force us to look at ourselves more deeply – to consider who we are. This can be a prelude to our taking charge of our life, beginning the long, painful, slow journey to being an individual:

> In his ignorance of his own despair a person is furthest from being conscious of himself as spirit. But precisely this – not being conscious of oneself as spirit – is despair, that is to say spirit-lessness . . . the despairer is in the same situation as the con-

sumptive; he feels best, considers himself to be healthiest, can appear to others to be in the pink of condition, just when the illness is at its most critical. (CUP 75)

So Kierkegaard wants to challenge and question the person who appears happy on the surface, who seems to lead a successful life, who has all the outward marks of what the world considers success. He wants these people to slow down, to be still, to look at themselves in a different way; and then, perhaps, they may come to recognize the façade they have constructed and the despair in which they actually live. Bringing people to this point is not easy – it will not be achieved by lecturing or criticizing them. It will not be achieved by persuading them to read more or to take a degree in philosophy or psychology. All these can merely be new forms of activity which prevent the individual looking closely at him- or herself. Kierkegaard is passionate about bringing people to a state in which they actually address the question of who they are, but he recognizes that subtlety is needed to do this. They have to be brought to recognize something that they do not want to recognize. They have to be brought to think in ways they do not want to think; they must be forced to look behind the masks they have constructed when to do so means feeling the despair they do not want to feel. To achieve this Kierkegaard employs what he terms 'indirect communication'.

Kierkegaard did not wish to found a new philosophic school; he did not see himself as an innovator. He was the fire chief who, when a fire breaks out, takes charge of proceedings. The matter is urgent, time is short and action is required. The fire chief may forcefully point out what needs doing but, in the matter of your own life and death, the response is down to you, 'that solitary individual' to whom this book is dedicated.

1

Kierkegaard's life

Søren Kierkegaard's father, Michael Pedersen Kierkegaard, was born in a poor village in Jutland where he suffered from cold, hunger and loneliness. One day, at the age of 11, Michael Pedersen was on the wild Jutland heath caring for cattle. He was alone, cold and wet and, because of his sufferings, he stood on a little hill, raised his hands to heaven and cursed God, who was so cruel as to allow him to suffer so much. The memory of this curse was to remain with him for the rest of his life. His uncle rescued him by taking him to Copenhagen to work in his clothing business. He eventually inherited his uncle's fortune, built up a successful cloth and trading business and became a wealthy man. He married at 38 and retired from business at the age of 40. His wife died two years after the marriage, and before the accepted mourning period was complete, on 26 April 1797, he married again – to Ane Sørendatter Lund, who had been a servant in the house before his wife's death. The first child was born on 7 September 1797 – four months after the marriage. Søren was the last of seven children from the second marriage.

Søren Aabye Kierkegaard was born on 5 May 1813 in Copenhagen, Denmark's small capital city. He died there on 11 November 1855. A brother and sister died before he was nine years old and his two remaining sisters as well as one of his brothers died before he was 21. Kierkegaard's father had a great influence on him as a child – although there is no reference in Søren's writings to his mother, who did not appear to be at all important in the family. Kierkegaard's father was a melancholy man who developed, after his retirement, a passion for philosophy. He would have friends in to dinner and they would discuss philosophy (mainly German) into the night. Kierkegaard used to sit and listen to the conversation and was fascinated by the swings in the argument. It was his father who helped develop Kierkegaard's imagination, taking him by the hand and walking him

1

up and down inside the house talking to him and conjuring up in his imagination the streets of the great cities of Europe, the father pointing out all the sights, sounds and smells to the young boy.

At school, Kierkegaard was always the odd one out, partly because he was physically weak, and partly due to his dress. His father made him wear shoes rather than boots like the other children, as well as skirts to his coat. He was nicknamed 'Choirboy', because his clothes resembled those of children in the charity schools, and also 'Søren Sock' because of his father's previous occupation. He had a devastating wit and used this instead of physical strength to protect himself from the jibes of his fellows. The Dean of Vibourg, who was at school with Kierkegaard, told a story which illustrates his personality:

> Professor Mathiessen, the teacher in German, was an exceedingly weak man who never had any authority over us. Once when the horseplay in class had gone very far – it was quite wild in all his classes – when the pupils had made a complete meal with butterbread, sandwiches and beer and had toasted one another with formal *prosits*, Professor Mathiessen was about to go out and report the affair to the Headmaster. The rest of us surrounded Mathiessen with prayers and fair promises, but Søren said only, 'Please tell the Headmaster that this is always what goes on in your class' – whereupon Mathiessen sat down and made no report. (Quoted in Walter Lowrie, *A Short Life of Kierkegaard* (Princeton: Princeton University Press, 1943), 50–1)

Kierkegaard's religious upbringing was rigorous and old-fashioned. As he describes it in *Point of View on my Life as an Author*:

> As a child I was strictly and austerely brought up in Christianity; humanly speaking, crazily brought up. A child crazily travestied as a melancholy old man. Terrible! What wonder then that there were times when Christianity appeared to me the most inhuman cruelty. (Quoted in Lowrie, *A Short Life of Kierkegaard*, 39–40)

Kierkegaard entered the Royal Guards for his military service but was discharged after three days as medically unfit. At the age of 17, in 1830, he entered Copenhagen University. He worked hard, particularly in the first year, enjoying the exploration of ideas, and read widely. He seemed happy, thoroughly enjoying university life, loving the theatre and the pleasure of conversation and being at the centre of so many parties: he appeared to be making a determined effort to break loose from his rigorous upbringing. He was popular – although people were nervous of him, as his wit could be cruel. He was one of the intellectual and cultural luminaries of Copenhagen society and was known to everyone. At the age of 20, in 1833, he began his *Journals*, which represent one of the most extraordinary such undertakings ever published and which give marvellous insights into his thought. His wide-ranging university reading contrasted with the conventional but highly orthodox religiousness of his home. His attention to his studies waned and he ran up considerable bills – which his father had to settle – as he lived the life of a wealthy young 'man about town'. His apparently carefree life, however, contrasted with feelings of deep depression.

Then, in his twenty-second year, what Kierkegaard referred to as 'the great earthquake' occurred. This may refer to one of two things – either to his discovery of his father's childhood curse or else to his discovery that his father had seduced his mother while she was a servant in his house soon after, or even before, the death of his father's first wife. Both would have had a considerable effect on Kierkegaard, as he had considered his father to be the model religious man. It was this event that Kierkegaard saw as marking the transition from youth to adulthood and it also put a 'distance' between him and his father which was not bridged until shortly before his father's death on 8 August 1838. Kierkegaard had a profound religious experience some months before his father died. He dated his report of this experience precisely – 19 May 1838, 10.30 a.m.:

> There is such a thing as an indescribable joy which glows through us unaccountably as the Apostle's outburst is unexpected: 'Rejoice, and again I say Rejoice!' – Not a joy over this or that, but full jubilation, 'with hearts and souls and voices': 'I rejoice over my joy, of, in, by, at, on, through, with my joy' – a heavenly refrain, which cuts short, as it were, our ordinary song; a joy which cools and refreshes like a breeze, a gust of the trade wind which blows through the Grove of Mamre to the eternal mansions. (Quoted in Lowrie, *A Short Life of Kierkegaard*, 124)

'The Grove of Mamre' is a reference to Genesis 18.1: 'The Lord appeared to him by the oaks of Mamre, as he sat at the door of his tent in the heat of the day.' Kierkegaard does not, however, dwell on this experience a great deal. It happened and it was part of his journey towards being a Christian but, looking back at the end of his life, he thought that throughout the whole of his life he was being educated into what it was to be a Christian.

Following the death of his father at the age of 81, Kierkegaard became a wealthy man and inherited a substantial house in Copenhagen. He was preparing for his theological examinations and passed these in July 1840. In 1837, before his father's death, he had met a very young girl, Regina Olsen, and had fallen in love with her, but she was only 14 and too young to be wooed and he had to work at his studies. She was confirmed in 1840 at the age of 16 and this was the recognized stage at which he could approach her. He was deeply in love and possibly also saw that Regina provided the hope of a normal life for him. He proposed to her and was accepted. However, he began to suffer from tremendous melancholy and increasingly felt that he could not go through with the marriage. We cannot know the precise reasons but it was at least partly due to his unhappy childhood, the secrets of his dead father, his own personality and the task in life he felt he had to undertake – he loved her too much to submit her to a marriage which he thought would make her unhappy. Finally, after much agonizing, he sent back the engagement ring with this brief letter:

> In order not to put more often to the test a thing which after all must be done, and which being done will supply the needed strength – let it then be done. Above all, forget him who writes this, forgive a man who, though he may be capable of something, is not capable of making a girl happy.
>
> To send a silken cord is, in the East, capital punishment for the receiver; to send a ring is here capital punishment for him who sends it. (Quoted in Lowrie, *A Short Life of Kierkegaard*, 138–9)

Regina was desolated and begged him to have her back – he could not explain why he would not, because he loved her too much. He believed that only by showing himself to be a scoundrel could she turn away from him and be free to love someone else. Otherwise she would have clung to him and would not have been free to find happiness elsewhere. Kierkegaard was convinced that Regina could not find happiness with him and because his love was so great he could not want anything else. He continued to love her for the rest of his life – so much so that one glance from her sent him to Berlin for five months. She later became engaged to a former teacher and she and Kierkegaard had no real communication thereafter. When Kierkegaard died, he left her everything he had.

Kierkegaard defended his thesis, 'On the Concept of Irony', in September 1841. In November, he left for the first of four visits he was to make to Berlin – on this first occasion he attended the lectures of Friedrich Schelling, a German philosopher and friend of Hegel. For the rest of his life Kierkegaard lived alone, with a servant, and had no close friends and dedicated himself to his writing. He loved walking the streets of Copenhagen and talking to people and also much enjoyed the company of his young relatives, to whom he was a figure of some amusement and whose visits were keenly anticipated. He was a well-known figure in the city and in the years from 1841 onwards lived an apparently carefree life, often being seen at the theatre. It was, however, something of a double life. He would sometimes go to the theatre at the interval just to be seen and when the next act started he would slip back to his rooms to continue his writing far into the night.

Between 1842 and 1845 he produced some of his most important pseudonymous works – *Either/Or, Repetition* and *Fear and Trembling* (1843), *Philosophical Fragments* and *The Concept of Anxiety* (1844) and *Concluding Unscientific Postscript* and *Stages on Life's Way* (1845), although at the same time he was also writing some of his greatest *Edifying Discourses* – sermons designed to be read aloud. In December 1845 he became involved in a public and very bitter dispute with the *Corsair* – a rather scandalous newspaper that defied the strict censorship of its time and relied heavily on gossip about the wealthier classes – which he decided to attack and which in turn attacked him. The upshot of this was that in early 1846 he was made into a figure of fun in Copenhagen, with the *Corsair* producing caricatures of him and making fun of his bandy legs so that he could no longer walk the streets without being mocked.

Kierkegaard continued his writing, but with a change in style and approach, and his books became more obviously religious. In 1847 he published *Works of Love* and *Edifying Discourses*, in 1848 *Christian Discourses* and in 1849 *The Lilies of the Field and the Birds of the Air* and *Three Discourses on Communion on Fridays* as well as, under the pseudonym Anti-Climacus, *Sickness unto Death* – which harks back to issues he had dealt with in earlier works. This was followed, in 1850, by *Training in Christianity*. In 1849 he also wrote *Point of View on my Life as an Author*, although this was not published until after his death. This book attempted to explain his authorship and what he was trying to do. Throughout this period he was a regular and committed churchgoer and wrote numerous sermons – he even considered taking a post as a pastor.

From 1849 onwards he became increasingly disillusioned with the established Danish Church, which he considered unfaithful to Christian discipleship. He lived in increasingly difficult financial circumstances, as he had been supporting himself all his life on his father's money and had earned little from his books. In 1854/5, shortly before his death, he directly attacked the Danish Church and its ministers in a series of bitter articles, including some published in his own broadsheet, the *Instant*. These articles have been collected together in a book titled *Attack upon Christendom*. He also ceased going to church and on his deathbed refused to receive communion from a minister who he considered to be a state employee rather than a servant of Christ – he would have liked to have taken communion from a layperson but that was not possible. He died in November 1855, giving thanks to God, looking forward to eternity and completely at peace.

Kierkegaard's lonely childhood; his melancholy and religious father, who was highly intelligent yet deeply affected by his cursing of God on the Jutland heath; his father's love for his first wife and his seduction of a housekeeper and his preoccupation with philosophy; Kierkegaard's active imagination, his unhappy childhood and the way he was made to stand out from his fellows and to hone and develop his wit and irony to protect himself; his dissolute life in Copenhagen once he left home; his rapprochement with his father and his religious experience; his engagement to and love of Regina and the stifling of his love for her; his few friends and his cruel treatment at the hands of the Copenhagen crowd following the *Corsair* affair; his unusual appearance and his loneliness – all these can be invoked to explain his writings in psychological terms; or they can be seen positively – because freedom from external distractions such as friends, security and family laid him open to discovering what it means to live in a relationship with God.

Kierkegaard himself would have considered the details of his life as irrelevant, and to concentrate on Kierkegaard rather than his message is to miss the point. It is, therefore, with his message and his thought – and not with his motivations or his psychological state – that the remainder of this book is concerned.

2

Faith and reason

Kierkegaard was a Christian theologian and philosopher writing in Denmark, a country where almost everyone was Christian and almost everyone went to church. He wrote, therefore, in a cultural milieu very different from ours. One of his central objectives was to examine the relationship between religious faith (particularly Christian faith) and reason. This was a theme that underpinned much of his writings. One important way in which he tackled this relationship was to look at the nature of Christian claims to truth; he did this from the perspective of a pseudonymous author who adopted the viewpoint of a relatively dispassionate philosopher. He was concerned not so much to determine whether Christianity was true but to unpack the logical consequences which would follow *if* it was true and thereby clarify the relationship between faith and reason. Initially, he did this in a book called *Philosophical Fragments* written in 1843, in which he contrasted the figures of Jesus and Socrates.

Many today regard Jesus (like Socrates, Gandhi, Martin Luther King, Nelson Mandela and others) as a good man who showed us how to live a good life. In an increasingly secular world, this is a widely accepted and appealing picture. It recognizes the goodness of Jesus, it recognizes his commitment to love, compassion and forgiveness, but it avoids the rational difficulties which many people feel are caused by claiming that Jesus is God, the second person of the divine Trinity. Putting it philosophically, the issue is whether Jesus is in an ontologically different position from Socrates. Was he a wonderful human being, just like other rare but remarkable human beings, or is there something different in Jesus' very nature?

Kierkegaard sets out, as a philosopher and theologian, to address this question, which lies at the heart of the claims made by traditional Christianity – but his aim in doing so is to explore the faith–reason debate. This was an important issue in the nineteenth century because of the work of two major philosophers. First, Immanuel Kant had argued that reason must be given pride of place and rationality must underpin the human understanding of morality and also of God. Religion, he claimed, must operate 'within the limits of reason alone'. Following Kant (who died in 1804) the increase in scientific knowledge had placed greater and greater emphasis on the priority of reason and Kierkegaard wanted to challenge this priority. Second, and even more influential by the time Kierkegaard was writing, was Hegel. Kierkegaard read Hegel with care and eventually reacted negatively to many of his central claims. According to Hegel, ideas develop through history; what is 'true' changes over time and depends upon a process of argument, on how we perceive things. Like Kant, Hegel emphasized the primacy of reason in accessing 'truth', and his approach was accepted by almost every philosopher of his day. Kierkegaard rejected it.

Socrates and Jesus

The story of Jesus is well known while that of Socrates is less so. Socrates was proclaimed by the oracle at Delphi to be the wisest man in Athens. When this was reported to him he could not understand it as he felt that he knew nothing. Socrates, therefore, set out to prove the oracle wrong and he did this by questioning those people who thought themselves wise about the source of their wisdom. During the course of this questioning, it rapidly became clear to Socrates that those who thought themselves wise were in fact not so. Their answers were confident enough to begin with but, under Socrates' close examination, it soon became apparent that they had few grounds for their claim to wisdom. Socrates therefore came to the conclusion that what the oracle was really saying is that that person is wisest who knows that he knows nothing.

Socrates acquired a delighted youthful following who much enjoyed seeing their revered elders being shown to be a good deal less wise than they first appeared. This of course made Socrates highly unpopular and in due course he was brought to trial on the twin charges of 'corrupting the young' (because he helped young people to think for themselves) and 'atheism' (because he rejected the anthropomorphic gods of ancient Athens). By custom, five hundred of the free citizens of Athens were allowed to vote on the guilt or innocence of the accused. Socrates' friends tried to persuade him to hire skilled orators who were trained in the best techniques of persuasion. These orators prided themselves on being able to sway the crowd and this was decisive for an acquittal. Socrates, however, totally rejected this idea, as the orators' approach was to suggest that 'truth' depends on how people perceive things, on a process of argument. Socrates knew that a trial which employed orators had nothing to do with the search for truth: the free citizens of Athens who would eventually vote would be swayed to accept the popular and the easy every time, and would therefore have no basis at all for their claims for true wisdom and learning.

We have a record of the trial written by Socrates' friend and pupil Plato, a dialogue called the *Apology* – although how much of this is historically accurate and how much is Plato putting his own thought onto Socrates' lips we cannot know. We do know, however, that Socrates, as recorded in the *Apology*, presented a reasoned and well-argued defence which seems to be irrefutable intellectually. However, the crowd were persuaded by the prosecuting orators to vote for conviction, which carried the death penalty. It was open to Socrates to propose some lesser punishment such as banishment or a substantial fine, and Socrates' friends tried to persuade him to do this as it was likely that such a plea would have been accepted. Socrates, however, refused, saying that any such proposal would represent a confession of guilt, and as he was not guilty he could not agree. The sentence of death was thus confirmed and Socrates was required to drink hemlock. He was allowed some time, however, before he took the drug and in another dialogue, the *Phaedo*, Plato records Socrates' last conversations with his friends. Socrates is given the chance of escaping from the city but he refuses to do this, claiming that he has lived all his life under the laws of Athens and will not reject them now. According to these laws he has been condemned to death and he therefore accepts the sentence. The *Phaedo* ends with Socrates taking the hemlock while his friends mourn: Socrates is calm throughout and engages in quiet philosophic speculation with his friends about what happens after death.

The parallels with Jesus are obvious – although given the account of Jesus in Gethsemane, Jesus may have faced death less calmly than Socrates. Are, then, Socrates and Jesus to be considered as broadly similar? It is with this question that Kierkegaard is concerned in

Philosophical Fragments, one of his earliest books. In some ways *Philosophical Fragments* is a book about Christology as it addresses the question of who Jesus was. Is Jesus simply to be considered as a remarkable man, able to provide real insights into the human condition and how life should be lived, or is he something more and, if so, what difference does this make?

Philosophical Fragments was written from the perspective of the pseudonymous character of Johannes Climacus, whose views are not necessarily Kierkegaard's, but are opinions that Kierkegaard has an interest in exploring, as it were, from the inside. Johannes Climacus represents an author who is attempting a philosophic analysis of Christianity but does not himself profess to have faith; he 'writes' both *Philosophical Fragments* and *Concluding Unscientific Postscript* from this point of view. Socrates, Climacus believes, is a human teacher relying on reason. Once human beings learn something, it really does not matter who taught them. Socrates is part of the whole, vast human enterprise which, over the centuries, gradually develops greater and greater knowledge about the universe and how it works. With each generation, the frontiers of our knowledge are extended by human endeavour. Some few individuals may be decisive in breaking through barriers of understanding at particular points, but the human race as a whole is contributing to the development of human understanding of the world. If one person fails to make an important new discovery or fails to provide a crucial insight, then someone else will, in the fullness of time, make the discovery or provide the insight.

Johannes Climacus' task in *Philosophical Fragments* is to examine the consequences *if* Jesus Christ is radically different from Socrates or any similar man or woman. Climacus certainly does not attempt to prove that Jesus is different and indeed, regards such an exercise as impossible. He merely seeks to examine the consequences *if* there is an ontological difference between Jesus and all other human beings. He begins with this as a possibility and, in *Philosophical Fragments,* attempts to tease out the possible consequences for the faith–reason debate.

In the case of a philosopher, scientist or other thinker, the moment at which someone comes to understand truth and the individual through whom this understanding is reached are both largely irrelevant. Any teacher is no more than a midwife (a comparison both Kierkegaard and Socrates make), helping the learner to come to knowledge. Just as when a woman gives birth it is the woman and the baby who are most important, so it is with the individual and coming to understand truth. A midwife is, of course, very helpful in the birthing process but if one midwife is not present then another can take her place. Similarly if one human teacher is not present, another can fulfil a similar role. Newton is acclaimed for discovering the fundamental laws of gravity but if he had not done so, then someone else would have made the discovery in due course. If Copernicus had not discovered that the earth revolved round the sun, then Galileo would have been the first to make the discovery – but the discovery would still have been made. Human beings are rational and can use reason to discover truths about the universe we inhabit. If, however, Jesus is essentially different from Socrates then Jesus is not like any other human being who happens to discover truths about the human condition. Jesus is not just another rational philosopher who might, perhaps, be a bit more intelligent than others. If Jesus is, as orthodox Christianity proclaims, God incarnate, then the teachings of Jesus may be expected to reveal something that mere human intelligence could not arrive at. So, Kierkegaard concludes, *if* Jesus is God, then various things follow:

1. The truth that is revealed in Jesus' life is not like that of Gandhi or Socrates – Jesus, as God, can reveal Eternal Truths (note the capital letters) which cannot be revealed in other ways.

2. The incarnation, in which God became human, is a decisive event in human history. It is not merely a matter of another baby being born who affected the world in a major way. *If* Jesus is God, then Jesus' birth is the moment when God decisively intervenes in creation.

3. If this is true, then for an individual to come to accept the message of Jesus is not like acquiring one more piece of information. It will have a decisive impact on the individual which will affect the whole of his or her life.

4. The moment when a person accepts the incarnation and decides to take seriously the Eternal Truth that Jesus brings will be decisive. It will affect the individual's whole life. It marks the passage from error to Truth. If Jesus is God and if the message that Jesus brings is decisive for all human beings, then Jesus is effectively the Teacher (note the capital letter) as he brings Truth that could not be known

elsewhere, and the Saviour of those who take on board that message as he brings people from error into Truth. Previously they were in error as they were working with a human understanding of truth, but when they accept Eternal Truth they move out of error.

5. Kierkegaard also equates error with sin. If Jesus is indeed God then a refusal to accept this is to be in error. It is to assert the primacy of human reason and to refuse to accept a revelation that goes beyond reason. If someone moves from refusal to accept that Jesus is God to an acceptance of this, then this is a move from error to Truth, from sin to faith.

6. For Kierkegaard, therefore, sin is *not* the opposite of virtue, as many suppose. Sin is a refusal to accept the truth of the Christian message – assuming, of course, that this message is true, and Kierkegaard accepts that there is no proof of this. Faith is a willingness to trust that God has intervened in human history out of love for human beings and to accept the message of love that Jesus brings – the message that God wants human beings to enter into a two-way love-relationship with God.

It is important to recognize all the 'if's in the above points. To repeat what has been said previously, Kierkegaard is not seeking to prove these statements to be true but merely indicating the consequences that follow logically from the claim that Jesus is God. Whether or not this claim is true is a separate issue. If Jesus Christ was just bringing people to see truths that they could have worked out for themselves given the necessary ability and insights, then Jesus would not be essentially different from Socrates. If he is different, then the Truth that Jesus brings must be of a different order which brings people from a state of being in error to an understanding of Eternal Truth which is not available elsewhere:

> The truth then is that the learner owes the Teacher everything. But this is what makes it so difficult to effect an understanding; that the learner becomes as nothing and yet is not destroyed; that he comes to owe everything to the Teacher and yet retains his confidence; that he understands the Truth and yet that the Truth makes him free; that he apprehends the guilt of his error, and yet that his confidence rises victorious in the Truth. (PF 38)

Eternal truth and Socratic truth

If Jesus Christ is the Teacher, then the individual who comes to know the Truth through him must be the learner. If Jesus Christ is decisively different from Socrates, then the Eternal Truth which he brings can be Truth which would not otherwise be available to us, of a radically different kind from Socratic truth. Eternal Truths are not truths we can come to learn on our own account. Human beings need help to gain access to these truths; they have to be revealed. What is more, they are a different type of truth from normal, object-ive knowledge. Eternal Truth has to do with what it is to be a self, what it is to be a human being.

The effects of sin

Kierkegaard considered that *if* Jesus Christ was indeed the God-man, then he did not simply provide Eternal Truth by living and dying on a 'once and for all' basis. God also teaches today, in our own time, through the Bible and can thus speak directly to the individual. Kierkegaard came from an Augustinian and Lutheran background and he believed the effect of sin on human beings to be profound. Modern philosophers in the Reformed Christian tradition such as Alvin Plantinga and Cornelius Van Til speak of 'the noetic effects of sin' – in other words the effect of sin on human abilities to know eternal truths. However, for Kierkegaard, sin is connected to the human assertion that unaided reason can work out what it is to be a human being and how to live in relation to God.

This confidence in reason does not take into account a point that Kierkegaard emphasizes – the Truth that Jesus reveals is not a matter of doctrines or propositional knowledge, it is Truth about human beings and their relationship to God. Reformed Epistemologists tend to overlook this and to concentrate instead on doctrinal statements such as the claim that God exists, yet, in one way, theirs is a helpful manner of expressing Climacus' point. If the Christian story is true, human emphasis on reason has deprived people of the condition necessary for them to accept Eternal Truth and only God can restore this condition and also communicate this Truth. Anyone who does not accept the Truth (assuming it is true) is in error – and this error is due to sin. The sin is due to a human refusal to accept that reason is not supreme and that faith may call people beyond reason.

What is not so clear is whether Climacus is referring to individual sin or to the Fall, whereby the whole of humanity has been affected by original sin. Both approaches give rise to difficulties. On one reading of the text, Climacus appears to be referring to individual sin:

> In so far as the learner was in Error, and now receives the Truth and with it the condition for understanding it, a change takes place within him like the change from non-being to being. But this transition from non-being to being is the transition we call birth. But now one who exists cannot be born; nevertheless, the disciple is born. Let us call this transition the New Birth . . . the disciple who is born anew owes nothing to any man, but everything to his divine Teacher. (PF 23–4)

On this view, the individual appears to have the potential to understand Eternal Truth at birth, but loses it by his or her own action or by his or her refusal to have faith. On this interpretation, questions can be asked about when this loss takes place. It must, however, be remembered that Kierkegaard is not using 'sin' here to mean what most people mean by the word. Sin is not moral failure but the assertion of the primacy of reason and, therefore, a refusal to accept the Christian revelation. The individual, on this model, loses the potential for understanding Eternal Truth, the condition for having faith, by relying on reason and coming to believe in its primacy. Such people need to have their potential to understand restored by being helped to see that faith can go beyond reason. Unless this is accepted then, for Kierkegaard, understanding the Truth is impossible.

Christ's coming to reveal Eternal Truth is decisive as it restores the condition or the possibility of faith to all human beings and is also a way of communicating Eternal Truth. Jesus confronts the power of reason to have the last word and, in doing so, opens the possibility for faith.

Sin

Sin, therefore, represents the assertion of the primacy of reason and, therefore, the rejection of the possibility of faith, since faith requires reason to be put into second place. Original sin has given human beings the false impression that they are able to apply reason successfully to the mystery of God. It is, perhaps, not a coincidence that Adam and Eve's problems started when they ate from the tree of knowledge. Karl Barth held a view not dissimilar to this.

Kierkegaard's pseudonymous character, Johannes Climacus, believes human beings and God to be separated by a great gulf due to error and sin and this chasm has to be bridged. What is more, the chasm is infinitely wide – after all, God is God, the creator of the universe, and human beings are very limited creatures in comparison. Human beings are in space and time; they are part of a created universe which they can only dimly comprehend. We are only beginning to come to some limited understanding of the reality of the nanoworld or, more significantly, of the world of quantum science, yet God is not another object in the universe of which both nano-reality and quantum phenomena form part. God is not a being in space and time. God is, therefore, inaccessible to human reason in the way that, for instance, the quantum world is not. Only God can bridge this enormous gap; human beings are impotent to do so. The incarnation achieved the bridging of the chasm; God chose to become a man and revealed Eternal Truth through language and an example which we can understand.

The love of God

Climacus asks why, if God exists and if there is an infinite divide between God and humans, God should choose to bridge the gap. The God of Aristotle was the unmoved mover, the uncaused cause who had no interest at all in the spatio-temporal universe. What motive could that God have to overcome the vast difference between God and human beings? What could move God, since God cannot be moved by anything outside himself, and has no needs that must be satisfied? Kierkegaard's answer is that there could only be one motive – love. This idea of God being motivated by love and, indeed, essentially being love is also endorsed by the Franciscan approach to theology and set out by St Bonaventure.

To illustrate his point, Climacus tells the parable of a king who was riding through a forest. He came across a small hamlet and stopped for some water. He was served by a humble village girl who enchanted him. He spent time talking to her and realized that he had fallen in love with her. The king faces an immediate problem if his love is genuine – how can he bridge the great gulf between himself and the girl so that genuine love can be possible? The king does not seek blind obedient service – he does not wish to take her to his bed and use her. He seeks a genuine love-relationship, and if love is to occur the girl must be free to reject or to love him for himself. This is not possible when the king is seen as a king and the young girl as a humble, uneducated maiden – the gap between them is too wide. There are two possible ways the great gulf between the king and the girl can be bridged:

> The king might have shown himself to the humble maiden in all the pomp of his power, shedding a glory over the scene, and making her forget herself in worshipful admiration. Alas, and this might have satisfied the maiden, but it could not satisfy the king, who desired not his own glorification but her. It was this that made his grief so hard to bear, his grief that she could not understand him. (PF 36)

The girl would be overwhelmed by the king's majesty: she would be awed, terrified and obedient, but love would be impossible. This way of bridging the gulf is therefore not an option. However, there is an alternative. The king could go to the girl in the appearance of 'The lowliest of persons. But the lowliest of all is one who must serve others' (PF 36). Thus the king, out of love, must go to the girl in the form of a servant and must hope that the girl will love him for himself – and not for his power and glory. Of course he runs a risk: he risks the girl not loving him. However, only if the king makes himself equal with the girl does love become possible. There are parallels with the marriage of Prince Charles and Diana Spencer. Diana was a young, naïve girl of 17 with little experience of the world. When Prince Charles set out to make her his bride – partly because she met all the requirements (she was a virgin from a good family with no doubtful past behind her) – she was unable to distinguish between the man and the Prince – and disaster ensued. Bridging the gap is not easy.

The analogy is obvious and Climacus spells it out clearly. God comes to earth as a human being, out of love. If the Christian story is true, then Jesus Christ is essentially different from Socrates, Gandhi or any other great religious leader since only he is God, only he can reveal the Eternal Truth. The incarnation is decisive as it bridges the gulf between man and God. This story is also helpful in showing the type of truth that God wishes to communicate – the king does not want the girl to learn objective facts about himself, he wishes her to fall in love with him. On this understanding God does not wish human beings to learn theological doctrines but to enter into a genuine love-relationship with God.

The idea that Jesus, an ordinary-looking man walking around Palestine nearly two thousand years ago, could also be God, the creator and sustainer of the universe, is not a reasonable one. God is the unknown, the absolutely unlike. As Kierkegaard says:

> There is an infinite, radical, qualitative difference between God and man. (J 697)

Humans make the mistake of conceiving God in anthropomorphic terms. God, Kierkegaard maintains, is qualitatively different from human beings – God is not the highest superlative of the human. The dangers of failing to take the unknowability of God seriously can scarcely be overestimated, according to Kierkegaard:

> The fundamental derangement at the root of modern times . . . consists in this: that the deep qualitative chasm in the difference between God and man has been obliterated. (J 6075)

The Absolute Paradox

The Jesuit theologian Karl Rahner referred to God as Holy Mystery – indeed Rahner's guiding motif was the nearness of God as Mystery and Kierkegaard's emphasis on God as the Unknown is not alien to this. If God is the Unknown, the absolutely unlike, how can God become man? How can the infinite and the finite meet? How can the Eternal and the temporal, the Creator and creature become one? Rationally and logically this idea must be rejected – and many today reject Christianity for precisely this reason. Jesus may indeed be considered to have been a wonderful man, a great ethical teacher, a religious inspiration – but he cannot rationally be held to be God, or so Climacus claims. Climacus believes that the traditional Christian claim about the incarnation, that Jesus Christ was both fully God and fully man, cannot be rationally understood or accepted. This, however, does not mean that it is not true. It is a paradox – it is, in fact, the Absolute Paradox, as it is the bringing together of two things which are most unlike, God and man:

> The supreme paradox of all thought is the attempt to discover something that thought cannot think. (PF 46)

There are two possible reactions to the Absolute Paradox: the first is offence and the second is faith. Confronted by the Absolute Paradox, reason will collide with it, will wrestle with it, will consider it – and reject it. Reason (philosophy) will take offence at the paradox and stand aside from it and Kierkegaard considers that it is entirely *reasonable* that it should do so. In a later work, *Training in Christianity*, written under the pseudonym 'Anti-Climacus', which he used to explore the perspective of somebody who himself had faith and who also 'wrote' *Sickness unto Death*, he says:

> Offence has essentially to do with the composite term God and man, or with the God-Man. . . . The God-Man is the paradox, absolutely the paradox, hence it is quite clear that the understanding must come to a standstill before it. (TC 83, 86)

Today, many philosophers of religion in the UK and North America operate firmly within a Kantian frame – religion must remain within the limits of reason alone. If this happens, then the traditional claim of the incarnation will be rejected. According to reason, the claim that Jesus is both fully God and fully man is *not* logical and if reason reigns supreme it should be rejected. The rational individual will therefore take offence at the Absolute Paradox and reject it because it is a paradox, because it offends against reason, 'because it is absurd' (PF 52). If reason is supreme then there is nothing more to say – reason can only reject that which goes against reason.

Johannes Climacus expresses the point succinctly:

> When the reason takes pity on the Paradox, and wishes to help it to an explanation, the Paradox does not indeed acquiesce, but nevertheless finds it quite natural that the Reason should do this; for why do we have our philosophers if not to make supernatural things trivial and commonplace? (PF 66)

It might appear from what has been said so far that faith is a question of the individual will. The individual must decide for him- or herself whether to set reason aside and to accept the Absolute Paradox. However, Climacus maintains that this is only part of the picture – faith is crucially a gift, given by God. That said, Kierkegaard does not accept the seemingly logical consequence that some are given faith while others are not. He rejects predestination and determinism and believes passionately in the freedom of each individual. Faith is a gift, but it is a gift that has to be received and striven for as well. It is as if two poles meet, just as two persons meet in a relationship. Precisely how these polarities come together, however, Kierkegaard does not explicitly specify and, indeed, the relationship between faith as a gift and faith as something that has to be striven for is one adopted by many major theologians including Aquinas, Luther and Barth. Kierkegaard's position, therefore, is faithful to the mainstream Christian tradition, although the tension between the two elements is not more easily resolved because of this.

Although Kierkegaard was by no means the first to make the claim that faith goes beyond reason, his great genius was to work out the consequences of this. Part of his tremendous contemporary relevance is to argue that reason is not paramount. Rational philosophy does not reign supreme – there is something higher and that is faith. Tertullian asked: 'What has Athens to do with Jerusalem?' and St Paul says: 'We preach Christ crucified, to the Jews a stumbling block and to the Greeks foolishness' (1 Corinthians 1.23). If offence is the response of reason to the Absolute Paradox, then there is another response as well – faith. Faith involves the commitment of an individual's life in a subjective relationship with God. When faith is absent, all that the individual will see when considering the figure of Jesus is an extraordinary man. Kierkegaard maintains that, if the Christian story is true, there is much more to the figure of Jesus than this.

Kierkegaard is a profoundly religious author and he uses his philosophic skills to try to bring individuals to see for themselves what Christianity involves and what it requires – but this is essentially a matter for each individual. Climacus puts it well:

If anyone proposes to believe, i.e. imagines himself to believe, because many good and upright people living here on the hill have believed, i.e. have said that they believed, . . . then he is a fool. (PF 129)

Whether or not the individual will respond to the Christian claim is a matter that he or she must decide, but the individual, Kierkegaard maintained, should respond on his or her own account and not because of the influence of a third party or a social group. A person today may be brought up in a Christian culture or may hear the Christian message, but this in itself will not be enough to engender faith – faith is something that must be accepted or rejected individually. Faith, like love, is essentially something that involves each individual: a person ought not to fall in love because another says it is a good idea and nor should a person have faith on these grounds.

A contemporary of Jesus and someone living today ('the disciple at second hand' as Kierkegaard terms him) are in exactly the same position. Both have access to certain information about Jesus – the one by observation and the other by reading the New Testament and by hearing about the Jesus story from others. It is true that one of Jesus' contemporaries may have had more factual information than the person who is alive today, but more factual information is not going to make the difference between faith and offence, between acceptance and rejection of the Absolute Paradox. Judas, the Pharisees and even St Thomas had first-hand knowledge of Jesus, but they did not accept that he was God – this is an individual step of faith. It is a commitment to, an acceptance of, Truth, a new birth. Clearly these are all identifiable Christian categories but they are categories that dominate *Philosophical Fragments* and which form a crucial part of the mosaic which Kierkegaard's thought represents.

To sum up, therefore, Kierkegaard argues that *if* the Christian story is true, then any merely human teacher (like Socrates) is in an essentially different position from Jesus. Jesus, as God, reveals truths that would not otherwise be accessible. The claim that Jesus is both God and man is, however, not *reasonable* – it will elicit either offence or faith. The truth of the Christian claim cannot be arrived at by reason since faith in the Absolute Paradox is actually beyond reason. This is one of the most important of Kierkegaard's ideas – that faith is higher than reason. Many today will reject this, yet it is at the heart of Kierkegaard's understanding of reality.

We will find that the theme of the relationship between faith and reason runs throughout Kierkegaard's works and that he consistently argues that faith needs to move beyond reason. This, of course, is something that much modern philosophy would never accept, but Kierkegaard considers this crucial.

Having raised the issue of faith and the related issue of truth, we must now consider how Kierkegaard deals with these issues.

3

The nature of truth

As noted in the previous chapter, Kierkegaard wrote *Philosophical Fragments*, which discusses the possible difference between Socrates and Jesus, in 1843. He regarded this as much the more difficult book to write than what is generally regarded as his principal work of philosophy, *Concluding Unscientific Postscript*, completed two years later. This book is also written under the pseudonym Johannes Climacus. At the end, Kierkegaard makes Climacus' standpoint clear:

> The undersigned, Johannes Climacus, who has written this book, does not give himself out to be a Christian; he is completely taken up with the thought how difficult it must be to be a Christian. (CUP 545)

Climacus sets out a critique of traditional ways of understanding truth, all of which claim that it can be known objectively through reason. As we saw in the previous chapter, Kierkegaard believed that complete and Eternal Truth is inaccessible to reason and that if we hold fast to reason then we may be led to believe that there is no ultimate Truth. Faith goes beyond reason; it is called to accept something which reason would reject, that reason is itself limited. The objective approach makes the individual irrelevant, as nothing is staked on objective facts – they need not affect an individual's life. We can study science, history, theology, psychology or philosophy and may build up much objective knowledge but this does not really get us very far. We may know more or less, live more or less 'successful' lives, but in the end such 'knowledge' cannot affect death or make much difference to the way we live. Learning cannot help us to understand the Eternal Truth or lead us nearer to the faith which, if it is true, could change everything. Faith requires an individual to stake his or her life on a claim that reason would reject – that reason itself is limited and there is something bigger, something Eternally True. It is not a single decision, it is a commitment to living and thinking differently, it is the beginning of a relationship and relationships are essentially subjective. There is a certain illusory comfort in certainty but it is illusory and commitment to the claim that reason cannot understand the Truth precludes it. Either the commitment continues or it does not. There can be no half-measures. Faith cannot depend on tests or be affected by arguments. It is a subjective state of being.

The claim that Jesus was God and man is the Absolute Paradox which cannot be understood by reason and cannot be established by historical enquiry. The most that any historical enquiry could establish is an approximation to the truth and there would never be enough certainty for the life-changing transformation that faith involves. Faith, for Kierkegaard, requires an inward transformation affecting one's very self and this is radically different from a simple acceptance of factual propositions. Faith requires a transformation of the individual so that the whole of his or her life is lived in a new way, and this is avoided by the factual or objective approach to knowledge of religious truth-claims. Belief that God exists or even belief that Jesus is God is not the same as Christian faith. St James' epistle says: 'You believe that there is one God. You do well. Even the demons believe – and tremble!' (James 2.19). In other words the demons believe *that* God exists; they do not 'believe' in or centre their lives on God. I may believe that the world is round because I have been told this is the case and have seen photographs, but Christopher Columbus believed in the world being round and staked his life on it when he attempted to sail round a world which others considered to be flat.

In the film *Indiana Jones and the Last Crusade* (dir. Stephen Spielberg, 1989), Jones is seeking the Holy Grail – the cup from which Jesus is supposed to have drunk wine at the Last Supper with his disciples. He is captured by Nazis who are also seeking the Grail and his father is seriously injured. The only hope of saving his father is to find the Grail. Indiana Jones evades the Nazis and races down an underground cavern at the end of which, a secret map has told him, the Grail is located. He comes to a halt before a huge precipice of immeasurable depth. On the other side of this chasm is the Holy Grail. The map tells him that if he steps out over the chasm a hidden bridge will appear. He cannot test whether the bridge is there or not – he has to stake his whole life on his belief that the bridge exists though there is no guarantee that it does. Jones is required to have faith that the bridge exists. This is not simply intellectual faith. He has to stake his life on the existence of the bridge by putting all his weight on it. If the bridge does not appear he will fall to the bottom of the chasm and die. In a similar way, for Kierkegaard, faith requires individuals to stake their lives on a claim (the incarnation) that may or may not be true. Faith, therefore, is an existential act.

Objective and subjective knowledge

Various questions in life can be looked at either objectively or subjectively – for instance what it means to get married, what it means to die or what it means to pray. Objectively the first of these might involve consideration of the marriage service, the formalities involved, the legal implications and the like, while the second might deal with questions about whether a human person survives death, whether the soul alone survives or whether there is a new body, whether one retains one's memories and so on. However, such objective questions leave out the passionate interest of the individual in these issues and Kierkegaard considered that the really important issues were raised when these questions were addressed subjectively. For instance, what does it mean for me and the way I live my life that I shall survive death? What effect will this have on all my actions and how will my life be transformed? These are questions of a different order from objective questions. Columbus' whole life was affected by his belief that the world was round and Kierkegaard's point is that faith should have a similar, subjective impact.

People who are considered to be wise may accumulate much objective knowledge, but this knowledge is not necessarily religiously or existentially significant. Kierkegaard puts it this way:

> what is most difficult of all for the wise man to understand is precisely the simple. The plain man understands the simple directly, but when the wise man sets himself to understand it, it becomes infinitely difficult . . . the more the wise man thinks about the simple . . . the more difficult it becomes for him. (CUP 143)

Kierkegaard's complaint is against philosophers, theologians and others who busy themselves building up more and more learning and lose touch with the simple and what really matters. In particular they lose touch with the essential nature of faith. They fail to address the important issues, such as what it means to have faith and how having faith will affect them as single individuals. They can become so stuffed with theological or philosophical knowledge that they never get round to living the simple life of faith, without which 'knowing' about religion will get them precisely nowhere. Human beings busy themselves with worldly, temporal tasks and so lose interest in the real issue of how to live. Questions such as 'How should I live?' or 'What does it mean for me to have faith?' can with much learning mistakenly seem to become irrelevant. Kierkegaard thinks that most philosophers are good talkers and writers but fail to express anything significant with their lives. He argues that instead of listening to what philosophers write or lecture about, people should instead look at how they live and what their lives express. Their words are no real guide to what they consider really important – this is shown in how their lives are lived.

Instead of living in a world of words that have ceased to have any impact, philosophers, theologians and teachers should be judged by how they live. An individual's life is the best expression of what he or she believes – not the words that are said. Indeed, Kierkegaard wishes to bring people to be silent, to cease to take refuge in language and instead to consider who they are before God.

Theologians may reflect deeply and read many books. They acquire much knowledge, but this does not make them Christians. Kierkegaard puts it like this:

When the question of truth is raised in an objective manner, reflection is directed objectively to the truth, as an object to which the knower is related. Reflection is not focused upon the relationship, however, but upon the question of whether it is the truth to which the knower is related . . . Let us take as an example the knowledge of God. Objectively, reflection is directed to the problem of whether this object is the true God; subjectively, reflection is directed to the question whether the individual is related to something in such a manner that his relationship is in truth a God-relationship. (CUP 178)

Either/Or, not Both/And

At the time Kierkegaard was writing, the dominant philosophical system in Denmark was that of Hegel. Hegel had died in 1831 and his ideas were widely accepted in Denmark and elsewhere. Hegel considered that Christianity was to a certain extent true. His dialectical method saw truth emerging in human history and Christianity as a product of history, of the dialectic between Judaism and Graeco-Roman religion, and between what we might today call 'capitalist' and 'socialist' modes of living. Christianity emerged from the process of history and is continually affected by the process of history – the Roman Catholics reacted against the Orthodox, then the Protestants against the Catholics, then the Nonconformists against the Protestants and so the process goes on. For a Hegelian, philosophy is essentially superior to theology; it enables us to understand where we are and see that Christianity is struggling closer to truth. For Hegel, God, or Absolute Spirit, was not a being or spirit who created and sustains the universe. 'God' is the Absolute Idea, the process of truth being realized through the rationality of the human mind. Essentially Hegel reinterpreted the traditional idea of revelation and of Jesus' incarnation. God does not stand outside the universe and plan to reveal truths that he already knows to humans; rather, the universe *is* God going through a process of self-realization, and human appreciation of aspects of the truth is due to God realizing those aspects at that time. Hegel revered Christianity but saw it as no more than an expression of his philosophy of history. Truth was emerging through the development of reason. Christianity was to a certain extent true – it represented a stage in the emergence of truth, and it could be regarded as partly true and partly false that Jesus was God.

This position Kierkegaard totally rejected. Instead of Hegel's stress on a dialectical approach to knowledge, which effectively means embracing opposing positions, accepting that they could both contain elements of the truth and bringing them together into a new position which should contain a greater proportion of truth (portrayed by Kierkegaard as a position involving 'Both/And'), Kierkegaard proposes an alternative. He substitutes the disjunction 'Either/Or' (either Jesus was God or he was not). Hegel placed faith within reason whereas Kierkegaard argues for the primacy of faith over reason.

Hegel tries to explain away the Paradox of the God-man by saying it is to a certain degree true. Kierkegaard insisted that the Paradox has to be confronted and either accepted or rejected. Kierkegaard would have more respect for someone like Richard Dawkins, who is passionately committed to rejecting Christianity, or someone who is desperately conscious of their failings and of their inability to live up to Christian ideas, than with the person who does not engage with the issue of whether or not Christianity is true or even worse, as in the case of Hegel, with someone who reinterprets Christianity in a way which abolishes its paradoxical nature.

Hegel's philosophy made human individuals essentially irrelevant – in a constantly evolving world, nobody could ever know or live in total truth – whereas for Kierkegaard each and every individual was of supreme and paramount importance and the possibility of understanding Eternal Truth and living in a relationship with it is always open to us. This disjunction between Hegel and Kierkegaard is still present in Christianity, with Hegelian thought having given new philosophic impetus to an understanding of Christianity which emphasizes the primacy of the community or 'people of God'. This was also an Old Testament idea. God maintained his covenant relationship with a people, not a person; the prophets and kings had some individual importance as critics and leaders of the community who might influence behaviour, but the fate of the covenant and the practical consequences of God being at hand or distant was ultimately in the hands of all the people, not of individuals. Kierkegaard provides a contrast to the community-based approach by emphasizing the primacy of the individual and the individual's life of faith which, although lived out in the community, will result in just their salvation.

Kierkegaard recognized that the objective approach to truth has advantages, as it seems to have a security that is lacking in the subjective approach. If truth is merely what someone thinks is true, then the danger is that one may be convinced something is true when it is totally false. This is a recipe for madness, and Kierkegaard cites Don Quixote as an example.

Kierkegaard's point is that if truth is simply determined by what someone is personally passionate about (i.e. a 'merely subjective determination of the truth') then there is no way of distinguishing someone who is effectively mad or deluded (like Don Quixote) from someone who has faith. Many commentators on Kierkegaard have taken the phrase 'truth is subjectivity' to mean that if an individual wholly and passionately embraces and lives by a particular idea, then this idea will be true for him or her. They assume that Kierkegaard is dismissing the whole idea of objective truth and making the final determinant of truth a particular individual's subjective state. This type of approach was to give birth to a whole movement in philosophy called existentialism which, essentially, demanded that individuals should be 'authentic to themselves' and avoid bad faith or inauthenticity. It was this authenticity, some philosophers claimed, that determined the truth. This, however, is a travesty of Kierkegaard's position.

As can be seen from the quote above, Kierkegaard clearly recognized that just being passionately subjective about a particular claim to truth was not enough to make something true. People are passionate about a whole raft of ideas, from fascism, communism, racism and the existence of aliens to nationalism, but this does not make these ideas true. Kierkegaard says that anyone who simply embraces a 'particular, finite, fixed idea' is in danger of madness and he illustrates this with Don Quixote. Passion, subjectivity and inwardness do *not* make something true.

Kierkegaard's argument is essentially directed towards God and the incarnation of Jesus Christ. We have seen that Kierkegaard considered that *either* Jesus was God *or* he was not – but proof cannot be supplied either way. However, lack of proof does not mean that this central Christian claim is not true. Absence of evidence is not evidence of absence. Either it is true or it is not. The key issue is that for an individual simply to assent to the objective truth of the incarnation (by, for instance, saying the Creed or simply agreeing that the statement is true, or even by attending church services and reciting the creeds which say that the statement is true) does not mean that the person has faith. The objective truth of the incarnation (if, indeed, it is true) has to be believed in the face of the apparent absurdity of the paradox and 'lived out' in a life of faith. It has to be appropriated by the individual so that it affects the whole of his or her life. Until this happens, the truth does not become true for the individual, it remains 'at a distance'.

This point is well illustrated by C. S. Lewis in his Narnia story *The Voyage of the Dawn Treader*. He tells how Aslan, the lion, comes to Lucy when she calls him:

29

'Oh Aslan,' said she, 'it was kind of you to come.'

'I have been here all the time,' said he, 'but you have just made me visible.'

'Aslan!' said Lucy almost a little reproachfully, 'Don't make fun of me. As if anything *I* could do would make *you* visible!'

'It did,' said Aslan. 'Do you think I wouldn't obey my own rules?' (ch. 10)

Lucy's calling Aslan did not make it true that he was there – Aslan was not some creation of her imagination. However, until she called him and he appeared it was not true for her that he was present. Kierkegaard's point is that the nature of Christian truth is such that unless we relate ourselves to it subjectively, we cannot 'know' it. One cannot be 'told'; one has to come to 'see' for oneself.

Kierkegaard asks where there is more truth – in the objective or the subjective way. The objective way of seeking truth seeks to minimize risk; it is based on reason, proof and justification. The subjective way, however, is fraught with risk: because there is no objective certainty, because there is no proof that a subjective commitment is correct, there is a much greater degree of vulnerability. However, it is only in subjectivity that the individual becomes engaged with the truth as a human being; objectively he or she can stand removed from it and contemplate it neutrally, as a bystander:

Now when the problem is to reckon up on which side there is more truth, whether on the side of one who seeks the true God objectively and pursues the approximate truth of the God-idea; or on the side of one who, driven by the infinite passion of his need of God, feels an infinite concern for his own relationship to God in truth . . . the answer cannot be in doubt. If one who lives in the midst of Christendom goes up to the house of God, the house of the true God, with the true conception of God in his knowledge and prays, but prays in a false spirit; and one who lives in an idolatrous community prays with the entire passion of the infinite although his eyes rest upon the image of an idol; where is there most truth? The one prays in truth to God though he worships an idol; the other prays falsely to the true God, and hence worships in fact an idol. (CUP 179–80)

Kierkegaard's claim is *not* that by worshipping an idol passionately, belief in the idol becomes true. What he is claiming is that when dealing with God the crucial point is the manner of one's relationship with God. In other words, are you or are you not in a God-relationship? If you are in a God-relationship, then what you are related to is God whatever name you may give to it. Similarly the other way round – if you are not in a God-relationship, then whatever the name you give to whatever you say you are related to, you are not in fact related to it. When you live as if Jesus is God you don't change the fact that *either* he is *or* he is not – but *if* he is, you have demonstrated the reality of your faith and deserve to be seen as his disciple. If you merely say 'Jesus is God' and do not live the consequences then your faith is not real and *if* Jesus is God you have lived in error, in sin. For Kierkegaard, religion has to do with the individual living out a relationship with God. This is probably the cornerstone on which all Kierkegaard's writings are built. 'Essentially,' Kierkegaard says, 'it is the God-relationship that makes a man a man' (CUP 219).

If faith is to do with a relationship with God, then faith must necessarily be subjective. In many ways there are parallels with love. You do not determine whether you are in love by being able to talk about your beloved, by being able to describe him or her and explain his or her background and aptitudes. Instead it is your relationship with the person you claim to love that is decisive. Are you in a love-relationship? The same applies to God. The question for faith is, effectively, 'Is God at the centre of your life? Are you in a love-relationship to God?' You cannot answer this question by reciting theological doctrines or by pointing to the books you have read or the objective truths you say you believe. The answer is to be found only by looking inside yourself and seeing whether God is, indeed, at the centre of your life and whether the whole of your life is determined by and focused on the relationship with God.

Kierkegaard's definition of truth *and* of faith is this:

> An objective uncertainty held fast in an appropriation-process of the most passionate inwardness is the truth . . . without risk there is no faith . . . If I am capable of grasping God objectively I do not believe, but precisely because I cannot do this I must believe. (CUP 182)

The reference to 'objective uncertainty' is to the fact that God's existence cannot be proved nor can Jesus' status as God be justified. Both are matters of faith. Faith means staking one's life on something, with total passion, knowing that there is no proof and it is always possible one could be wrong. Faith necessarily involves risk: Kierkegaard describes it as being 'suspended over 70,000 fathoms' (CUP 183). The individual relies on faith alone and that places him or her in a very vulnerable position without the safety and security that are supposed to come with rational proofs. Yet think of it like this. In the film *The Truman Show* (dir. Peter Weir, 1998), Truman Burbank has lived in Seahaven for more than thirty years, a perfectly normal life, not realizing that his world is the set for a reality television show and everybody but him is an actor. For all we know, any one of us could be living like Truman – *either* we are *or* we are not – and we cannot prove that we are not. We have to decide how to live, though – *either* we live as if this world is a construct (and just imagine what that might mean) *or* we live as if our Seahaven is real.

It is not comfortable to think about this, to consider that there is no certainty that our friends and loved ones really care, that we really deserve praise and rewards, that what we are told is true, and yet we live as if these things are unquestioned. Thinking human beings should understand the state which Kierkegaard describes and appreciate, to some extent at least, his argument for the inadequacy of reason.

Faith is not adherence to a set of doctrinal propositions. Faith involves inwardness, it involves living out a relationship with God. A person cannot live out a subjective relationship merely by being part of a crowd or a group; each person has to live the relationship as an individual. The idea of being a Christian as a matter of course is a contradiction in terms. You cannot fall in love as a matter of course or be in love merely because you are a member of a society that talks about love.

Kierkegaard is rigorous in his approach – *either* Christianity is true *or* it is false. What it cannot be is a little bit true. *If* it is true then it demands that everything else takes second place to living out the relationship with God. If it is not, then it is irrelevant. Kierkegaard wishes his reader to face the challenge 'either all – or nothing'. If Christianity is true it demands nothing less than the whole of a person's life. If it is false, then it should be dismissed as irrelevant.

Pilate's question 'What is truth?' is a detached, objective question (cf. CUP 206). If he had asked the subjective question 'What, in truth, have I to do?' he would never have condemned Jesus. This latter question would have been a matter for Pilate's subjectivity and he could not have washed his hands of this sort of question.

The idea that 'truth is subjectivity' has considerable relevance in contemporary discussion of ecumenical questions. Inter-faith dialogue as well as dialogue between different Christian churches tends to concentrate on doctrines, rituals and similar objective matters. If Kierkegaard's approach to subjectivity is taken, then a very different position emerges. The issue then becomes whether individuals in different faith communities are or are not genuinely 'living in the truth' or living in a relationship to the absolute which Christians call God. A Muslim may call this absolute Allah and Hindus may see this absolute as having many different aspects. However, the Muslim, Hindu and Christian who are passionately trying to 'live the relationship' may have much more in common and be much closer to God than different Christians who may assent to the same objective truth-claims but who do not share the God-relationship. This will be dealt with in more detail in Chapter 10.

Faith and philosophy

If it is possible that Christianity is true, if it is possible that one day there will be a judgement, then the judgement will not be on what doctrines have been accepted but on how each individual has subjectively 'taken on board' and lived out his or her faith. 'As you have lived, so have you believed,' claimed Kierkegaard. It is not a person's words but an individual's life which is the best picture of faith. Faith, however, means being 'suspended over 70,000 fathoms' – in other words, it involves resting one's whole existence on something which may not, in the final analysis, be true.

To illustrate this, Kierkegaard tells the story of visiting a Copenhagen churchyard and sitting on a bench. Then, as today, there was a high hedge surrounding the seat on which he was sitting. He suddenly heard the voice of an old man very close to him behind the hedge who was talking to a child of about ten. He learnt that the little boy was the old man's grandson and they were standing by a freshly dug grave – that of the old man's son and the boy's father. It quickly became clear that the old man's son had abandoned his faith in pursuing philosophy and had then died. The old man's faith was his strength and hope, yet his son had thought there was something higher than faith and he had thereby sought and lost what was most important of all, and the father had been unable to communicate with him. Kierkegaard said:

> The venerable old man with his faith seemed to be an individual with an absolutely justified grievance, a man whom existence had mistreated because a modern speculation, like a change in the currency, had made property values in the realm of faith insecure. (CUP 216)

When a currency is devalued, it no longer represents a store of value. People who thought they had money suddenly find that they have nothing at all. Similarly people had faith and considered this a firm bedrock on which their lives could be built, but then philosophers came along and undermined their certainty, destroyed their foundations and derided their faith because it went against reason. Kierkegaard, however, argues that faith is the highest thing that any individual can attain. Modern speculative philosophy mocks faith and makes it out as something of no consequence which is held on to by the naïve and ignorant. This Kierkegaard refused to accept. If faith is the highest, then reason has no right to cheat people out of faith. It is not possible to go further than faith. Faith is the highest and most difficult demand. It is not something that one can achieve and then move on; it has to be lived out hour by hour, day by day, month by month and year by year for the whole of one's life. It is totally demanding, challenging, uncomfortable and lonely.

We have seen that, for Kierkegaard, truth is subjectivity in that subjective truth involves an individual living out a relationship with God and there is no objective proof of the validity of this relationship. Faith therefore involves risk. However, if Kierkegaard is not to succumb to the charge of relativism, he must provide some criteria for what it means to live in a relationship with God and how an individual can know that he or she is in such a relationship. This is dealt with in Chapter 8 – but prior to this it is necessary to look at Kierkegaard's stages of life.

4

The aesthetic stage

Kierkegaard analyses human life in some detail and argues that generally human beings who are reflective and thoughtful fit into one of three categories or 'stages' in life; the relationship between them is of central importance in understanding his whole corpus. In several books he uses love as the focus for looking at the relationship between the stages, and this analysis also throws light on his views on the relationship between men and women. The most significant books dealing with the stages are *Either/Or* (which focuses on the aesthetic and ethical stages) and *Stages on Life's Way*, although most of his work is relevant to an understanding of the stages.

The stages are not necessarily meant to be sequential (there is much debate on this issue among commentators), nor are most people entirely in one stage rather than another. Indeed Kierkegaard did not believe that most people were in any one particular stage. The stages represent different ways in which an individual may centre their life. In *Concluding Unscientific Postscript* he argues that 'existing' or thinking people drive through their lives: they are hitched to a horse and have a particular direction and mode of transport. Yet for many people life has no centre; they drift through life attracted by whatever momentarily takes their interest and fancy; they are subject to all the vagaries of fate and whatever their whim may be at a particular moment; they are often oblivious, unable to engage in self-analysis or understand where they are going. He wrote,

> the existing person is the driver, that is, if existing is not to be what people usually call existing, because then the existing person is no driver but a drunken peasant who lies in the wagon and sleeps and lets the horses shift for themselves. (CUP 311–12)

The unreflective life

Most people, therefore, are like drunks – they have no control over their lives and drift through existence. People who inhabit or seek to inhabit one of Kierkegaard's three stages are in a very different position. Being in any one of the stages places an individual in a minority. People in the stages have reflected on life and life has a clear centre for them – but the stages differ in that there are radically different centres depending on which stage an individual is in. There are three stages – the aesthetic, the ethical and the religious – although there are also sub-categories of these.

Kierkegaard is a master of irony (as noted earlier, his thesis was on the Socratic concept of irony) and of indirect communication. His message is seldom obvious. Although he writes with great depth and subtlety about the aesthetic and ethical stages, it is important to understand that his primary purpose is to encourage people to see their barrenness and emptiness. He analyses these through pseudonymous characters who explore these stages, as it were, from within. In this and the next two chapters the three stages will be outlined.

Living in the aesthetic

The aesthetic stage is the focus of the first part of *Either/Or*, whose pseudonymous author claims to have found the letters described in the book in an old bureau which he bought – so the position of one in the aesthetic stage is developed through layers of ambiguity.

The person in the aesthetic stage rejects the ethical norms and the values of society and is instead dedicated to constructing his or her own identity in relation to his or her own desires. This could occur through living in the world of the intellect, achieving satisfaction by understanding and creating ideas and having these ideas praised and used by others. Kierkegaard labelled Kant and Hegel 'philosophers of the aesthetic' because he saw their cleverness being more about their own egos than about trying to understand and live in relation to Eternal Truths. He wrote,

> Prior to the outbreak of cholera there usually appears a kind of fly not otherwise seen; in like manner might not these fabulous pure thinkers [i.e. Hegel and his adherents] be a sign that

a calamity is in store for humankind – for example, the loss of the ethical and the religious? (CUP 307)

It could occur through the pursuit of pleasure, albeit pleasure of a sophisticated kind which feeds the ego rather than baser pastimes usually designed to block out thought and consciousness. The aesthetic life can be devoted to any temporal goal – power, money, reputation, hobbies – but above all, the person in the aesthetic stage must be in control of their own lives and must achieve by their own standards. The pleasures of the aesthetic have to be repeated again and again in order to sustain the enjoyment. One of the features of the aesthetic is the danger of boredom, which Kierkegaard sees as a part of the human condition – in much the same way as Pascal saw human beings constantly seeking to flee from boredom and, later, Sartre described the endemic state of *ennui*. 'Doses' of pleasure, like those of addictive drugs, need to be repeated and gradually increased in order to attain the same level of satisfaction.

Love in the aesthetic stage

Kierkegaard uses seduction as an example of the way that the aesthete loves, but this is no more than a good example, albeit one that illuminates other areas of Kierkegaard's thought. Therefore, his focus on love should not be taken to mean that this is the only way the aesthete can attain pleasure.

Plato's *Symposium* is a discussion on love and Kierkegaard has a similar dialogue called 'In Vino Veritas' which appears in his book *Stages on Life's Way*. It is set at a banquet where a number of people state their views on women (I am grateful to Gregor Malantschuk's excellent book *Kierkegaard's Way to the Truth* for his insights into Kierkegaard's discussion of women). Plato takes his discussion on love in the direction of the higher, spiritual understanding of love whereas Kierkegaard moves in the opposite direction – towards the denial of the Eternal and immersion in the Temporal. There are five characters in Kierkegaard's dialogue, who speak in turn; three of these Kierkegaard uses elsewhere as pseudonymous authors:

- the Young Man
- Constantin Constantinus (author of *Repetition*)
- Victor Eremita (the hermit, author of *Either/Or*)

- the Fashion Designer
- Johannes the Seducer (author of 'Diary of a Seducer' in *Either/Or*)

The Young Man sees the erotic relationship between men and women as amusing. People devote their whole life to love of another; their individuality is taken over yet no one can define what love is:

> Who would not feel alarmed if time and again people suddenly dropped dead around him or had a convulsion without anyone being able to explain the reason for it? But this is the way erotic love intervenes in life ... since erotic love expresses itself in loving a one and only, a one and only in the whole world. (SLW 36)

Love is meant to be spiritual, yet it is motivated and consummated by physical desire, which is largely selfish. The two lovers want to come together to form one self, yet this is an illusion. Worse than this, the erotic leads to marriage, which is the supreme example of 'society' taking over the individual:

> at the very same moment the species triumphs over the individuals, the species is victorious while individuals are subordinated to being in its service. (SLW 43)

The Young Man sees contradictions everywhere in the married state. People drift into marriage and the responsibility this imposes. Their individuality is denied and they are obliged to conform to society's values. This leads him to reject any positive relationship with a woman.

Constantin Constantinus is the host of the banquet and he speaks second. He considers women to be made merely for relationships:

> It is the man's function to be absolute, to act absolutely, to express the absolute; the woman consists in the relational. (SLW 48)

Constantin is amused at the power women exert over men:

> [Men] regard her as an absolute magnitude, and make ourselves into a relative magnitude. (SLW 51)

Women are creatures of whim and of pleasure – looked at ethically they do not have an identity of their own but seek their identity in relation to others. They seek to 'lose themselves' in a husband or in children.

Victor Eremita believes that women should never be taken seriously. Any man who takes a woman seriously becomes tied in to foolishness and unpredictability. However, women do have advantages – they can evoke genius, heroism, poetry and sanctity *provided* that the man does not attain the woman he desires. If he does, then he is lost. Marriage, Victor maintains, is devoid of meaning and drags an individual down: it leads inevitably to mediocrity:

> A positive relationship with a woman makes man finite on the largest possible scale. (SLW 62)

The best way for a woman to awaken her husband to an ideal would be to die or to be unfaithful to him.

The Fashion Designer thinks that the whole of a woman's life revolves round fashion:

> If one wishes to know women, one hour in my boutique is worth more than days and years on the outside. (SLW 66)

His primary motivation is to make women so ridiculous that they get bound in chains which corrupt her much more effectively than if she was simply seduced (SLW 70). The Fashion Designer's aim is to prostitute women by making them slaves to fashion. He says to the other characters:

> Do not go looking for a love affair, stay clear of erotic love as you would the most dangerous neighbourhood, for your beloved, too, might eventually wear a ring in her nose. (SLW 71)

Johannes the Seducer proclaims that his life is devoted to pleasure:

> Anyone who, when he is twenty years old, does not understand that there is a categorical imperative – Enjoy – is a fool. (SLW 72)

As one might expect, he sees woman's only function as satisfying man's desire. Woman is the greatest enticement in the world and most men succumb and become bound by a woman in marriage. He, the Seducer, is one of the small band of 'happy lovers' who have their pleasure without permitting women to tie them down – they always nibble at the bait but are never caught (SLW 84). Johannes speaks in praise of women; in fact he considers them to be 'more perfect' than the male:

nothing more wonderful, nothing more delicious, nothing more seductive can be devised than a woman. (SLW 76)

Women want to be seduced and the devotee of erotic love wants to respond to this by loving as much as possible. No woman is like another:

> For what else is woman but a dream, and yet the highest reality. This is how the devotee of erotic love sees her and in the moment of seduction leads her and is led by her outside time, where as an illusion she belongs. With a husband she becomes temporal, and he through her. (SLW 80)

In the 'Diary of a Seducer' (in *Either/Or*), Johannes sets out the Seducer's position as well as his technique. His aim is to maximize his pleasure in the pursuit of a young girl, Cordelia. The pursuit is carried out in great detail – there is no rush to bed but a carefully planned and executed entrapment which the Seducer intends to bring him maximum enjoyment on the journey. The seduction is prolonged as long as possible and when, eventually, he makes love to Cordelia (having first persuaded her to agree to become engaged to him and then breaking the engagement) he loses all interest; the 'fun' of the chase is now over and he wants nothing more to do with her. His sole concern has been his pleasure and, he might say, to teach her that she should pursue a similar aim and not seek to 'lose herself' in him or in others.

Kierkegaard's pseudonymous character in *Stages on Life's Way*, Hilarious Bookbinder, portrays three modern female characters, Marie Beaumarchais, Donna Elvira and Margrethe, as representing a typical feminine desire to be 'won' by a man who will remain faithful, and contrasts this to Don Juan, who has the opposite ambition. To seduce all girls is the masculine expression of the feminine yearning to let herself be seduced once and for all with heart and soul. It is easy to see from this why Kierkegaard can be portrayed as holding women in contempt, but this is radically to misunderstand him. He is writing under pseudonyms and giving the perspectives of different aesthetes who have immersed themselves entirely in the temporal and a search for pleasure which they recognize as transitory. Despair is the inevitable outcome of this position and, coupled with this, other human beings will be regarded in what Kierkegaard considers a totally false light. Far from praising any of the above positions, therefore, Kierkegaard is actually trying to show their bankruptcy. Having said this, he would feel that many women do fall into the categories set out above. Like it or not, there are women whose only desire is to marry and to be 'won' by the one true love for the whole of her life, just as there are men who see women just as objects of pleasure. However, this is radically different from saying that *all* women or men fall into these categories, still less that they should do so.

Some commentators say that Kierkegaard's pseudonymous characters do not represent his own views. This is certainly true in part. He uses these characters to take perspectives other than his own. However, echoes of the pseudonymous thought can be found in Kierkegaard's private journals. Certainly the pseudonymous authors put forward a distinctive point of view, but from that point of view Kierkegaard would endorse what is being said:

> what is said by The Seducer (in 'In Vino Veritas') about woman being bait is very true. And strange as it may seem, it is nevertheless a fact that the very thing which makes the seducer so demonic and makes it hard for any poet to contrive such a character is that the form of knowledge he has at his disposal embraces the whole Christian ascetic view of woman – except that he employs it in his own way. He has knowledge in common with the ascetic, the hermit, but they take off from this knowledge in a completely different direction. (J 4999)

The aesthete as well as the hermit are similar in that they recognize that their identity is to be found in the inner world rather than through convention. They both see the threat that marriage as an institution represents – however, their reactions are very different. The aesthete feels in the grip of fate, which is beyond his or her control; and, above all and whether he or she knows it or not, the aesthete is subject to despair. The 'happy' and the 'unhappy' aesthete alike end in despair: the happy aesthete (such as Johannes or Don Juan, who represent unreflective masculinity and 'success' in terms of pleasure) ends in despair because constant immediate doses of pleasure can never satisfy. Such pleasures are always transitory, always pointing forward to something else which also does not satisfy. The unhappy aesthete, by contrast, feels the immediate absence of pleasure and also despairs.

The aesthete may come to recognize that whatever he or she does will end in disillusion, although this may not happen: many aesthetes continue to live their lives without facing the realization that they are in hidden despair. Experience teaches the aesthete to avoid all commitment, as he or she learns that commitment will always disappoint and is transitory. However, this lack of commitment results in emptiness and boredom, which a person may try to relieve by increased 'doses' of pleasure, which simply make the position worse. Recreational drugs today might be a good example, but there can be many others. In 'The Rotation Method' in *Either/Or* Kierkegaard sets out the prudent aesthete's position, which is dedicated to avoiding entanglements:

> Watch out for friendship . . . Never go in for marriage. Married people promise to love each other for eternity. This is easy enough to do but it doesn't mean much, for when one is through with the temporal he will certainly be through with the Eternal as well. If, instead of promising eternal love, the parties concerned might say – until Easter, or until the first of May – this would make sense, for in this case both would actually say something and something which they might possibly stick to. (EO 243)

In the aesthetic stage, a human being sees himself as locked into the temporal and there is no way that this can end in anything but despair. Whatever happiness exists in the temporal world is transitory and illusory and whether this is recognized or not, despair will result. For the aesthete, love involves seeking to be loved – not loving. Gillian Rose maintains that Kierkegaard's book *Repetition* sets out the transition from being loved to being able to love. She puts it like this:

> Repetition would be the passage from beloved, loveableness, to love-ableness: from knowing oneself loved, 'loveable', to finding oneself graced with a plenitude of being-able-to-love, and thus to risk loving again and again, regardless of any particular outcome, disastrous or successful. To be love-able, to love singularly, to forgive, or release, and hence to love again and again, is the one thing the work can hardly speak. (*The Broken Middle*, 23)

As we shall see in Chapter 9, this is close to Kierkegaard's idea of non-preferential love, a giving love which seeks nothing in return.

This for Kierkegaard is the highest form of love – but it is not found in the aesthetic stage, as the person in that stage is essentially self-centred and selfish. He or she is thus incapable of either giving or receiving genuine love.

Judge William, who Kierkegaard's pseudonymous author of *Either/Or*, Victor Eremita, portrays as the paradigm of the ethical stage, also throws light on the aesthetic. He analyses the different types of aesthetic existence, all of which he rejects. The Judge suggests that at the first level the aesthete's motto might be 'live according to your desires' (EO 155), and the Roman emperors Caligula and Nero are cited as examples. At the second level the motto might be 'enjoy yourself', which Kierkegaard considers might be represented by living as an epicure. Next comes the aesthetic view which seeks detachment – effectively a stoical independence. In one way or another, these three forms of the aesthetic stage all see enjoyment, or at least prevention of pain for the self, as the main aim of life.

The demonic

Beyond this, however, is the person who has seen the bankruptcy of all forms of temporal enjoyment but who refuses to relinquish the aesthetic stage and persists in a way of living that he can control. Such individuals sink into their own despair and will not let go of it, although they refuse to recognize it and assert their own control over their lives. It is almost impossible to break out of this extreme stage of the aesthetic. The individual has built an immense protective wall round him- or herself and will allow nothing to penetrate this. It is this stage of the aesthetic which Kierkegaard describes as the demonic. The person in the demonic stage is self-aware, thoughtful and firmly in control of life. Nothing from outside can penetrate the iron-hard protective wall. There may be many reasons why a person may get to this state – they may have been hurt and discover that relationships disappoint; they may have never experienced love in childhood and therefore become self-protective; or they may simply come to the state of only being able to tolerate life if they are firmly in control and can manipulate their surroundings and relationships in ways they consider acceptable. Such a person may achieve a great deal in life. They are often strong and successful and people may admire them for their strength and independence. They may convince themselves that they are happy and content with life but, Kierkegaard believes, under this exterior shell – often very well buried – lies despair.

Those in the demonic stage may well be aware of God or the Eternal but realize that this provides the ultimate threat to their identity. Since to submit to God, to be obedient to God, would take control of their lives away from themselves they will utterly reject the possibility of God as altogether too threatening. Kierkegaard says that human beings

> are not willing to think earnestly about the Eternal. They are anxious about it, and anxiety discovers a hundred ways of escape. But this, precisely, is what it is to be demonic. (CA 157)

Such an individual is aware of God or the Eternal as a possibility and is repulsed by it: the Eternal is specifically rejected. The demonic is shown in closing itself off from and being repulsed by God, who represents the supreme good and the ultimate threat to the aesthetic's control and independence. This represents what Kierkegaard calls 'inclosing reserve', the wish of an individual to turn in on him- or herself and to reject God. The individual finds identity in opposing him- or herself to the divine. Kierkegaard explains the demonic in terms of Christ's contact with demons in the New Testament; the demonic is anxious about the good, convinced that Christ has come to destroy him or her, and implores Christ to 'go away'. Those suffering the demonic form of anxiety define themselves against the object which they dread, namely God or the Eternal. There is, then, a relation to the divine by the person in the demonic stage, but it is a relation of repulsion. In the parable of the Merman in *Fear and Trembling* there is a reference to him entering into an absolute relation to the demonic which represents complete rejection of the Eternal, thus

> The demonic has that same property as the divine, that the individual can enter into an absolute relationship to it. (FT 123)

The demonic stands at the opposite pole to the divine. A person in the demonic state is 'closed in' on her- or himself because this individual cannot bear to have her or his identity challenged by the divine. By living in the demonic stage, the individual stands outside the ethical – in a way similar, as we shall see in Chapter 6, to the person in the religious stage:

> By means of the demonic the [individual] would thus aspire to be the single individual who as the particular is higher than the universal. (FT 123)

This is an isolated position which cannot be achieved by 'going along with the crowd'. The person in this stage rejects obligations to human beings:

> the demonic can also express itself in contempt for men . . . his strength is his knowledge that he is better than all those who pass judgement on him. (FT 131)

The demonic is close to Nietzsche's superman, someone who thinks her- or himself superior to others, someone who can ignore the demands of ethics and society which seek to constrain him. To such a person both God and duty to human beings are essentially irrelevant – though for Kierkegaard the demonic, while acknowledging the existence of God, establishes her or his identity by rejecting the divine, whereas Nietzsche can be interpreted as rejecting the existence of God entirely.

Kierkegaard believes that the demonic person, just like the religious person, must have great strength of character, because strength is required to remain either in repulsion from or attached to God. It is a consistent position, a position which requires subjectivity and inwardness and which cannot be achieved by choosing to live by ethical norms. The stories of Don Giovanni and Doctor Faust (which Kierkegaard discusses in *Fear and Trembling*, 132ff.) express something of great importance which Kierkegaard recognizes. Both Don Giovanni and Faust are in the demonic stage – that is why Don Giovanni refuses to repent of his crimes even when he is held by the Commendatore and is being dragged off to hell. Both men define themselves against God and have so closed themselves off from God that they are unable to open themselves to the possibility of overcoming their state by relying on the divine. The choice lies between

1. maintenance of identity and being dragged to hell or
2. abandonment of their former identity by relying on God.

It is the latter step that Don Giovanni will not take. Effectively, such an individual cannot repent, as to do so means destroying the identity he or she has so painstakingly built up in opposition to and rejection of the divine.

Both Don Giovanni and Faust are individuals in that they have identified themselves by their rejection of God. They are extreme examples of the human effort to build individuality unaided. They do not drift with the crowd, they stand on their own – but they stand in opposition to the divine. They have turned themselves into the sort of people who are exiled from God and, in so doing, hell is the fate they have chosen. One of the key ingredients is *pride*: they have hung on in pride to their self-sufficiency and will not break out of it by relying, in humility, on God. The demonic is the ultimate stage of anxiety to be found in the aesthetic stage. In the final analysis, it will end in despair and the only hope is to be saved by the good, by submission to and reliance on God in faith. Don Giovanni is not in despair; on the contrary he has a restless energy and zest for life – he represents the full force of the sensuous which is fleeing from anxiety. But this energy and zest is grounded in the temporal, which inevitably must have an end, and it is when the barrenness of this is recognized that despair may result – as nearly happens to Don Giovanni when he is faced with hell. Just before he is dragged off to hell, he stirs up within himself a renewed zest for life which represents his very identity. This is the furthest point he can reach. Don Giovanni is forced out to life's most extreme point, where he insists on staying. He will go to hell holding fast to this position rather than destroy his self-created identity and repent.

In summary, the demonic is the ultimate stage of anxiety which is found in the aesthetic stage. In its final analysis, it will end in despair and the only hope is to 'be saved by' God. The difference between the demonic and someone who has faith is that although both are in an absolute relationship to the absolute, the demonic is in a relationship of total rejection. The demonic establishes her or his identity in relation to the divine and by rejection of it.

The demonic is shown in closing itself off from and being repulsed by the good. It represents 'inclosing reserve', the wish of an individual to turn inwards and to depend on him or herself alone and thus to reject any absolute beyond the human psyche. The individual finds identity in opposing him or herself to the divine.

Kierkegaard explains the demonic in terms of Christ's contact with the demonic in the New Testament – the demonic is anxious about the good, convinced that Christ has come to destroy him, and implores him to 'go away'. This definition of someone suffering the demonic form of anxiety means that demonics reject and define themselves against the object of dread. The demonic is 'closed in' because this individual cannot bear to have his or her identity challenged by the divine.

The whole aesthetic stage is utterly rejected by the person in the ethical stage – and it is to this stage that we must now turn.

5

The ethical stage

Judge William's rejection of the aesthetic in *Either/Or* is well argued and cogent. In place of the aesthete's lack of commitment, the judge praises the freely chosen commitment that the ethical stage represents. It is by the individual's own choice of the ethical that he or she integrates the self and establishes his or her identity. The individual, the judge claims, makes a free decision to commit him- or herself and then lives out this commitment. The individual is bound to freely chosen laws and God is not necessary. Judge William says:

> The choice itself is crucial for the content of the personality; through the choice the personality submerges itself in that which is being chosen, and when it does not choose, it withers away in atrophy. (EO 163)

Marriage as an example of ethical choice

Marriage is the paradigm of choice. A woman and a man enter into a freely chosen commitment to each other and then live out this commitment. In place of the aesthete's approach of 'using' women with a total lack of commitment, the judge offers the high and honourable estate of marriage and freely chosen love based on duty. The judge praises women particularly in their roles of wife and mother. This, he clearly considers, is the destiny of women, a message he continues to portray in *Stages on Life's Way*:

> Woman is more beautiful as a bride than as a maiden; as mother she is more beautiful than as a bride. As mother she is a good word spoken at the right time, and she becomes more beautiful with the years. (SLW 169)

The judge sees marriage as the paradigm of the ethical – acknowledged by society and of crucial importance to the community:

> Marriage is and remains the most important journey of discovery a man can undertake. Every other kind of acquaintance with existence is superficial compared to that acquired by a married man – for he and he alone has thoroughly fathomed the depth of human existence. (SLW 97)

Married love, in the ethical stage, is a high calling and is to be contrasted with the fickleness of love in the aesthetic stage, where there is no commitment. Marriage is not fickle as it is based on duty; it grows stronger with the passage of the years and the commitment shown to the public choice that was made in the marriage service. The judge admits that 'the first effervescent passion of falling in love' does not last, but marriage knows how to sustain this love (SLW 95). Marriage provides chains and bonds which, when freely accepted, are not only welcome but also provide the identity for the married couple:

> What I am through her she is through me, and neither of us is anything by oneself, but we are what we are in union. (SLW 93)

This is a good example of the role of the pseudonymous author in Kierkegaard's writings – this position rejects everything that Kierkegaard believed in, particularly the paramount importance of each person being a solitary individual before God. However, under the pseudonym, Kierkegaard can delineate this possibility and pretend to argue for it, hoping, of course, that his reader will see its bankruptcy. Love, according to this view, is essentially ethical duty – the duty to the freely chosen partner and to the children that result from the marriage. If the initial choice is strenuously maintained, as from an ethical point of view it must be, then this choice provides identity and meaning to the lives of the participants.

Baptism is another public ceremony in which the community puts its seal of approval on the birth of children. (When Kierkegaard was writing, of course, all children were baptized, just as everyone went to church each week; these were generally accepted social duties.) However, this easily becomes a substitute for the relationship with God which is essential. Kierkegaard is not rejecting the importance of Christian baptism nor of marriage, but he is drawing attention to the danger of the outward ceremony being substituted for the inner transformation that is required. For Kierkegaard, Christianity is essentially an affair of spirit and affects one's inmost self – it cannot be expressed in terms of outer convention.

The tragic hero

It is not easy to live ethically, to live not according to desire but according to ethical rules. Kierkegaard, in *Fear and Trembling*, calls a man who does this and who is called to make supreme sacrifices for the sake of duty a 'Tragic Hero'. He cites the examples of Agamemnon, Jephthah and Brutus – all of whom sacrifice the person they love to a higher ethical duty. Agamemnon, for instance, was the commander of the Greek fleet on the way to the siege of Troy when the fleet became becalmed. Lots were cast to determine who had brought this misfortune and the lot fell on Agamemnon's daughter. He had to sacrifice her for the good of his country. Someone who lives in the ethical stage lives according to rules which are understood but may still take great moral strength to live by: thus Agamemnon had to give up his ethical duty to his daughter for a higher ethical duty, namely his duty to his state. This moral strength comes from the individual, who refuses to give in to desire and instead does what is morally right.

Many Christians regard sin as acting immorally or unethically and would therefore see the ethical life as the highest aim for a human being. This is not Kierkegaard's view. He considers this to be essentially pagan, stemming from Aristotle. St Thomas Aquinas used Aristotle's philosophy to lay down an ethical code which has become known as natural law and which forms the cornerstone of Catholic natural theology. On Aquinas' view, to sin is to act unethically: to act against morality is to act against reason and also against God. Kierkegaard rejected this: he thought that this said no more than that duty to ethics was the same as duty to God, and once that was said, then any idea that there really was a duty to God evaporated. All that was left was a duty to ethics. As Kierkegaard's pseudonymous author Johannes de Silentio says in *Fear and Trembling*:

> The whole of human existence is in that case entirely self-enclosed . . . God becomes an invisible, vanishing point, an

impotent thought, and his power is to be found only in the ethical. (FT 96)

Moreover, for Kierkegaard, putting ethics at the centre led to despair; as he said:

> Every human existence not conscious of itself as spirit, or not personally conscious of itself before God as spirit, every human existence which is not grounded transparently in God, but opaquely rests or merges in some abstract universal [state, nation, etc.] or is in the dark about itself . . . every such existence, however outstanding its accomplishments, however much it can account for even the whole of existence . . . every such life is none the less despair. That is what the Old Church Fathers meant when they spoke of pagan virtues as splendid vices [Augustine, *City of God* 19, 25]. They meant that the heart of paganism was despair, that the pagan was not conscious of himself before God as spirit. (SD 77)

Ethics and conformity

For Kierkegaard, to live in the ethical stage is by no means the highest way of life. Indeed living the ethical life is all too often to lead a life of conformity, to conform oneself to the state, the community or, perhaps, the Church – *but not to God*. You may be living a highly strenuous life, you may be morally admirable, you may never offend against the moral code, but God is irrelevant. The attempt by one's own efforts to conform one's will to some chosen ethical norm ends in despair and in a denial of individuality because, essentially, that is to seek to conform oneself to the community, the group, the crowd. One may well be praised, admired and understood, but only in finite terms.

This is a surprising conclusion, as many Christians accept that sin is ethical wrongdoing and equate obedience to God with obedience to moral norms. They believe that the opposite of virtue is sin. But Kierkegaard specifically says:

> the opposite of sin is by no means virtue . . . No, the opposite of sin is faith which is why in Romans 14:23 it says 'whosoever is not of faith, is sin'. And this is one of the most crucial

definitions for the whole of Christianity: that the opposite of sin is not virtue but faith. (SD 114–15)

The ethical, with its personal choice of 'openness' and acceptance of society's values, even if these are regarded as equivalent to a duty to God, is for Kierkegaard no more than a path through which one may realize the bankruptcy of trying to come close to God by 'keeping the rules'. Such an approach, as Jesus recognized in relation to the Jewish Torah, is doomed to failure. Acknowledging this may open up the possibility for faith. For Kierkegaard, no individual self will be able to rest until it is in relationship with God rather than with temporal ends. Recognizing this and realizing that one is in a state of 'unrest' and disquiet can lead a person onwards towards faith. We have seen that faith means putting reason aside and accepting the Absolute Paradox; it means trusting in God in the absence of any proof. The life of faith is the life lived in relationship with God and, in *Either/Or*, Kierkegaard through his pseudonymous character is effectively trying to lead his reader to see that the ethical life as well as the aesthetic life will end in disappointment.

There are a variety of implicit pointers to this in the text when Judge William, while writing to the aesthetic Seducer and praising the virtues of the ethical, also warns of the dangers of having anything to do with truly religious categories. Real faith, for the judge, is impossibly strenuous, too lonely, too costly a path. The virtuous ethical life may require dedication but it is, essentially, a safe path which reason can understand and which everyone can applaud and appreciate. Marriage, although it may involve ethical striving, nevertheless also provides comfort and security.

Kierkegaard does not have a high view of marriage – this does not mean that he considers marriage incompatible with Christianity, but that it can only be compatible if the two parties are both true individuals. Ibsen's play *A Doll's House*, which illustrates the absolute nature of the 'all or nothing' demand and illustrates well the denial of individuality and individual development that marriage often involves, may well have been based on Kierkegaard's work.

Too often, Kierkegaard considers, the demands of society and conformity, the social expectations that come from raising children, setting up home and the like, become a substitute for individuality and the God-relationship. This he sees as a travesty of the Christian demand. He blames this on priests and the general wish for medio-crity. As Thoreau later wrote in *Walden*, 'The mass of men lead lives of quiet desperation' – there is a demand by 'the crowd', the mass of people, to live an ordinary, unexamined and passionless life in which God is essentially irrelevant, and yet they want this life to be regarded as Christian. When such a person comes to the end of his life, 'one thing has escaped him; his consciousness has taken no note of God' (CUP 219).

Either/Or, despite appearances, is essentially a negative book. Kierkegaard uses his pseudonymous mouthpieces to point to the ultimate barrenness of both the aesthetic and the ethical, leaving the way open for what Kierkegaard effectively considers the true end for every human being – the religious.

The individual before God

Many contemporary philosophers, and indeed theologians, see ethical obligations to the community as higher than religious obligations. Kierkegaard considers the ethical stage to be dangerous precisely be-cause it is the category of the crowd, the community. All too easily, the ethical may not allow a person to attain individuality, and with-out individuality people easily lose any sense of their own direction, lose the centre of their lives and revert to being dragged around like drunken peasants. If this happens then they cease to 'exist' in any positive way at all. Kierkegaard is forthright in his condemnation of anyone who thinks they can approach God as a member of a club or group – essentially, Christianity is a matter of inwardness and therefore the concern of each individual.

Although some may reject the aesthete's way of life, the aesthete is at least trying to be an individual and, as such, may be brought to the point of despair, where he or she is faced with two alternatives – to remain locked into him- or herself or to submit humbly to God. It is this possibility, and the decisive transition from despair to faith, which, for Kierkegaard, is most important of all. The person in the aesthetic stage may be closer to God than the person in the ethical stage because he or she at least is alone and isolated and has begun to take him- or herself seriously – this, in turn, may lead to despair and the need for faith. Despair is possible in both the ethical and the aesthetic stages, but it is easier for the ethical to provide an apparent and illusory security (Tolstoy's novella *The Death of Ivan Illich* is a good illustration of this point).

Judge William portrays a complacency and confidence in the ethical choices he has made that was anathema to Kierkegaard; only as an individual, alone and isolated from the crowd, can true identity be found. Despair may finally pull the individual to her or his true home – which can only be found through the 'narrow gate' of humility and trust in the Eternal. *Either/Or* is designed to bring its readers to see the bankruptcy of both the aesthetic and the ethical in order to prevent them from wasting their lives. As Kierkegaard puts it:

> So much is spoken about wasting one's life. But the only wasted life is the life of one who has so lived it, deceived by life's pleasures or its sorrows, that he never became decisively, eternally, conscious of himself as spirit, as self, or, what is the same, he never became aware – and gained in the deepest sense the impression – that there is a God there and that 'he' himself, his self, exists before this God . . . So many live their lives in this way . . . when the hour glass has run out, the hour glass of temporality, when the worldly tumult is silenced and the restless or unavailing urgency comes to an end, when all about you is still as it is in eternity – whether you are man or woman, rich or poor, dependent or free, happy or unhappy . . . eternity asks you and every one of these millions of millions just one thing: whether you have lived in despair or not. (SD 57–8)

Despair at the attempt to attain an identity by one's own efforts is the step before faith. *Either/Or* presents us with dead ends – the individual can only move beyond these dead ends by willing one thing: to belong to Christ. It is in this stage that Kierkegaard's comments about women can be seen in their true perspective. His negative comments only reflect what he saw as a truth: that most women and men do fritter away their lives. However, if they can be brought to see beyond this, the distinctions of gender vanish:

> In the relationship to God, where . . . a distinction between man and woman vanishes, it is the case both for the man and the woman that self-abandonment is the self, and that the self is acquired through self-abandonment. (SD 80–1)

Before God, human beings are individuals. This is the great equality and it is only before God that all outward distinctions vanish – a theme Kierkegaard continually takes up in *Works of Love*, a book to which continued reference will be made in Chapter 9.

6

The religious stage

Despair

Kierkegaard sees both the aesthetic and the ethical stages ending in despair. The person in the ethical stage has chosen to centre his or her life around an ethical code, in relation to a particular group of other people. This will end in despair – just as concentration on self ends in despair for the person in the aesthetic stage. The ethical good will come to be seen as a construct, which only appears to confer meaning and purpose, and will eventually be seen to be empty. An analogy might be that of a mother who centres her whole life on her family, sacrificing everything for their comfort and happiness. One danger is that she loses any sense of her own identity, becomes lost as a person and in common terms becomes a boring drudge. Another danger is that she works and works but her efforts go unappreciated. Her children rebel in an attempt to establish their own identities and, in the end, all her efforts cannot create a stable and unchangingly happy world at home. She becomes disillusioned and is filled with despair that she has achieved nothing. Ibsen examined such a situation in *A Doll's House*.

Only when the individual recognizes that there seems no alternative to despair and that all finite ends terminate in disappointment is it possible to relate him- or herself directly to God. Effectively, a person may be driven to God when all other alternatives fail – almost willy-nilly. Human beings learn to live behind the mask of public opinion, the identity they have constructed for themselves, and think that this gives them security. Once it is recognized that this mask is no more than a construct, and that underneath the 'happy and secure' exterior there is only emptiness, then the individual *may* begin – and it is only a possibility – to take the religious dimension seriously.

A relationship with God

The religious stage entails a personal relationship with God and a direct accountability to God – all finite ends are subordinated to this. Two steps are involved in the religious stage: first the subordination of all temporal ends, and second the focusing of the whole of an individual's existence on the relation to the Eternal. The second step involves the individual having an absolute relationship to the absolute or, in other words, acting as if God is the absolute and everything else is relative to this. Kierkegaard takes seriously the biblical assertion that, for God, what is not thinkable, what is least expected, is possible – but only through faith. Faith is always non-rational, it 'begins precisely where thought stops' (CUP 412).

If only the first step is taken, despair will again result. Resignation from all temporal concerns can be achieved by an individual's own efforts. Such an individual is a 'knight of infinite resignation', who surrenders all temporal aspirations and, in so doing, becomes conscious of being an individual before the Eternal – an 'eternal consciousness' comes into being when she or he becomes aware of God in freedom from the distractions of the temporal. However, the second step is the step of faith and, as we saw in Chapter 2, faith involves an action by God. It is not something that can be achieved simply by an act of human will. What is more, humility is an essential precondition for faith.

It is only when one is broken by despair, unable to rely on one's self and one's own strength, that real faith can arise. This is why despair is an essential precondition for faith. The person who is strong, doing well in the world and self-sufficient, will not come to faith. Pride and self-sufficiency are effective barriers to a relationship with God.

Kierkegaard maintains that the religious stage requires all worldly concerns (the temporal) to be subordinated to the centring of one's life on God. This does not mean becoming a hermit; rather it involves living in such a way that temporal matters are not of primary concern. Someone who takes this step may become materially comfortable and even successful, but this will not be important or significant to them – if all their possessions and reputation were lost, this would be of no real significance. Kierkegaard gives the example of Job, who loses everything and, gradually, comes to accept this. He regains the temporal trappings that he once lost but these are no longer of primary significance to him.

Suffering is a mark of the God-relationship – if someone really puts God into first place then this will inevitably lead to confrontation with the world and being misunderstood by others. This isolation is uncomfortable and lonely; to sustain the faith journey through the whole of one's life is precisely the task but it is incredibly arduous. It is much more 'sensible', much more 'rational', much more understandable and acceptable to conform, but this is precisely a denial of the God-relationship:

> The ethical constitutes the temptation; the God-relationship has come into being; the immanence of ethical despair has been broken through. (CUP 235)

To sustain the God-relationship, day by day, week by week and year by year, is demanding, and few people will be willing to take the lonely path that this involves. Just as being in love is a one-to-one relationship, so relating oneself wholly to God is something that can be done only between the individual and God. No one can relate to God by conforming to the crowd.

The established order, according to Kierkegaard, represented the accepted ethical and other conventions of modern society or even the Church. This established order is certain to be offended and to reject Jesus because his message is too uncomfortable and because he challenges the supremacy of reason. Those who live their lives by conforming to the expectations of their peers will also be offended:

> 'Why', says the established order, 'why do you want to plague and torture yourself with the prodigious measuring rod of the ideal? Have recourse to the established order, attach yourself to it. There is the measure. If you are a student, then you can be sure that the Professor is the measure and the truth; if you are a parson, then the Bishop is the way and the life; if you are a scrivener, the Judge is the standard . . . The established order is the rational; and you are fortunate if you occupy the position of relativity accorded you – and for the rest let your colleagues take care of . . .' 'Do you mean to say my salvation?' 'Why certainly. If with regard to this matter you encounter in the end some obstacle, can you not be contented like all the others, when your last hour has

come, to go well baled and crated in one of the large shipments which the established order sends straight through to heaven under its own seal.' (TC 91)

The established order of the Church maintains that provided one is a Christian as it understands being a Christian (possibly by baptism, confirmation, occasional church attendance and giving money regularly to the Church to sustain the standard of living of the priests) then this is all that is required. Secure as a member of the club, each individual will be shipped straight off to heaven after death. Kierkegaard thinks that this makes a mockery of God – each individual, on his view, must render a personal account for her or his life. Faithfulness to the God-relationship and how this has been lived out on a daily basis will be the foundation for the judgement of God.

It is now possible to see the different approaches to love in the three stages:

- In the aesthetic, love is essentially sensual or erotic and the person uses love to maximize her or his enjoyment. The purpose is to be loved and to enjoy this experience.
- In the ethical stage, love is essentially duty and is represented by freely chosen love within the family.
- In the religious, however, love is focused primarily on God and, because of that, on love of neighbour – it is a giving love. For Kierkegaard, a religious love is essentially a *non-preferential love* that does not favour any one human being over others.

Kierkegaard does not maintain that the religious stage rules out the sexual – but he does maintain that the sexual is such a powerful force that it can easily lead people away from the Eternal. As he puts it:

Here, as everywhere, I must decline every misunderstood conclusion, as if, for instance, the true task should now be to abstract from the sexual, i.e. in an outward sense to annihilate it . . . The task, of course, is to bring it under the qualification of the spirit (here lie all the moral problems of the erotic). (CA 80)

The problem, in other words, is how, if one lives a life centred on God, one can subsume sexual relationships under this category without the love that such relationships express becoming dominant.

Religion A and Religion B

Although, as outlined above, the religious stage is the third of three stages, in fact Kierkegaard distinguishes two distinct segments of the religious stage – Religion A and Religion B. Religion A has been outlined above: the individual recognizes the bankruptcy of the aesthetic and ethical, subordinates the temporal and looks to Christ as the prototype of the perfect human being, not as a personal saviour. This is a common position today – Jesus is seen as an extraordinary and wonderful human being who can be a good guide to how life should be lived, but nothing more than this. The individual, by an act of will, renounces the temporal in order to make room for the Eternal. The individual can take the step from the aesthetic or ethical to Religion A when the barrenness of the temporal is recognized; however, the step into Religion B cannot be made unaided. Gregor Malantschuk describes the step into Religion A as

> [doing] away with human self-reliance to risk oneself upon 'the seventy thousand fathoms' of water. This daring act is the beginning of the journey on the religious way. (*Kierkegaard's Way to the Truth*, 56)

There is, however, nothing specifically Christian in Religion A and it is in Religion B that the decisively Christian categories are found, with, in particular, the introduction of the idea of sin. The focus of Religion B is the Absolute Paradox of the God-man, which requires the abandonment of the supremacy of reason as well as the security found in the objective. It necessarily involves, therefore, the enormous risk of staking one's life on something which may be mistaken. Religion B is characterized by vulnerability as well as by an awareness of sin and the acceptance of forgiveness.

'Sin' is not a popular word today, but for Kierkegaard it was central. We can understand the rate of progress we are making on the road towards God by looking at the extent to which we are conscious of sin. The further down the road the individual travels, the greater will be the consciousness of failure before God and total dependence on God's love. All security is left behind, the individual's own strength is abandoned, and he or she lives by faith alone. Nowhere is faith greater than when it comes to belief in the forgiveness of sins, which is an absolutely essential part of Christian faith.

Faith is the condition necessary for the forgiveness of sins – Kierkegaard claims that people lightly skip over the idea of forgiveness,
but such people do not take the relationship with God or the Eternal
seriously. To those that do, forgiveness is nothing less than a miracle.
We are bound by our actions into the power of sin, and it is God's
action in the incarnation that is crucial in freeing us from its power.

Interestingly, this was a view that Immanuel Kant had already
recognized in *Religion within the Bounds of Reason Alone*, although
few modern commentators dwell on this aspect of his thought. Kant
held that human beings make their own prisons by acting continually according to inclination and desire rather than according to
reason. If this pattern is repeated continuously then reason eventually loses its power to control the individual and the individual
enters a prison of his or her own making created by personal desire.
Kant held that human beings can only be released from this state of
'radical evil' through the grace of God (they cannot release themselves;
they must be released by God). It is the incarnation and the example of Jesus' life and death which demonstrates the strength of God's
love and gives humans a glimmer of hope that they may receive his
grace, though never the belief that they might deserve it. Kant notes
that without the demonstration of God's love there would be only
despair. Kierkegaard is making a similar point. Faith is the acceptance
of being loved by God; it is far from easy and there is always the possibility that one might be wrong – but the individual stakes his or
her own life on the possibility that God exists and will save them.
For Kant, though, it is not possible rationally to accept that God could
love and save a sinner; thus the fate of the individual is perhaps even
less comfortable than that of living in 'fear and trembling' or 'the sickness unto death'. Unlike Kierkegaard, Kant turns to the possibility of
creating a better world which could allow future people to avoid falling
into the trap of radical evil and thus to deserve salvation.

For Kierkegaard, however, there are forces acting to push and pull
the individual into faith. First is despair, which can push the individual towards God. The individual may come, through despair in
the ethical or aesthetic stages, to recognize that it is only in relation
to God that any security and hope can be found. Second, God, on
the other side, provides the gift of grace. Kierkegaard was adamant,
however, that 'cheap grace' must be rejected – grace comes only
when the individual is broken and in pieces; it is not an automatic

'freebie', given out like sweets to children. It is true that Kierkegaard considers grace to be a universal gift – but it is one that has to be accepted by the individual.

In Chapter 2 we saw that the opposite of faith was offence and offence is itself sinful. This is why the opposite of sin is not virtue but faith. Someone who cannot accept the forgiveness of sin is, essentially, someone who rejects the incarnation and this makes sin still worse. The individual chooses to remain in sin and rejects the paradox because it does not make sense (SD 113–24). She or he is offended by the Christian message and continues to give primacy to reason. Kierkegaard firmly rejects all objective certainty with regard to the truth of Christianity, in particular to leave room for faith and the gift of grace by God:

> depart from me, damned assurance! Save me, O God, from ever becoming absolutely certain. Preserve me in the hinterland of uncertainty so that it may always be absolutely certain that if I attain salvation I receive it by grace. (ED 218)

Religion A can be attained by an individual's own efforts. A person can will to give up all hope of the temporal and to be grounded in the Eternal. He or she can look to Christ as an exemplar but the transition from Religion A to Religion B occurs when the individual realizes that her or his own will is not sufficient and depends on Christ alone for forgiveness of sins and for salvation.

Faith and discipleship

As noted in Chapter 2, for Kierkegaard there is nothing higher than faith – which is why he was so angry with philosophers, priests and theologians who attempt to defraud people out of recognizing and aiming at it. It is very tempting for the individual to avoid the suffering that faith will bring and the commitment it entails, but faith is made more difficult by the ridicule and opposition of the crowd. Faith therefore requires isolation – it necessarily involves a lonely path, walking hand in hand with God alone and relying and trusting on God for the whole of one's life. One must accept being loved when one is acutely conscious of how unlovable one is.

Kierkegaard's pseudonymous character Johannes Climacus seeks to work out step by step, using philosophic reasoning, what faith amounts to (the name Johannes Climacus is taken from the Egyptian monk who wrote *The Ladder of Divine Ascent*). For Kierkegaard this is a particularly masculine way of proceeding and is to be contrasted with the way of love.

Johannes Climacus' delight is to begin with a single thought and then, by coherent thinking, to climb step by step to a higher one, because to him coherent thinking is an ascent to paradise. He is a rational, male philosopher investigating Christian faith and giving an account of it. Nowhere could there be a clearer statement of Kierkegaard's distance from his pseudonym. For Kierkegaard himself, philosophy and language in general can only serve to bring us to a place where words come to an end and when, as individuals, we are confronted by God. Love may be an expression of the confrontation but we will not arrive at the ability to love through philosophy.

Faith is, essentially, a life – a life lived in imitation of Christ and as a follower of Christ. It involves becoming a self, an individual whose life is informed by an awareness of one's dependence on and accountability to God. The 'admirer' of Christ is not the follower. Admirers can look on Christ objectively, they may talk about Christ, they may applaud him – but their admiration does not lead to following him day by day. Only the follower is the disciple. Kierkegaard puts this well in his parable 'Luther's Return', in which Luther comes back and challenges a religious writer (Kierkegaard may well have been thinking of himself here):

Assume that Luther has risen from the grave . . . assume that one day he addresses me and says 'Are you a believer? Do you have faith?' Everyone who knows me as an author will recognize that I am the one who comes out best from such an examination for I constantly said 'I have not faith' . . . However, I will not lay stress on this; for as all others call themselves Christians and believers, I also will say 'Yes, I am also a believer'. 'How is that?' replies Luther, 'for I have not noticed anything in you, and yet I have watched your life; and you know faith is a perturbing thing. To what effect has faith, which you say you have, perturbed you? Where have you witnessed for the truth and where against untruth? What sacrifices have you made, what persecutions have you endured for Christianity?' My reply: 'I can protest to you that I have faith'. 'Protest, protest – what sort of talk is that? . . . Bah, an end to this nonsense. What avails your protestation?' 'Yes, but if you would read some of my books, you will see how I have described faith, so I know therefore I must have it' . . . 'I believe the fellow is mad! If it is true that you know how to describe faith, it only proves that you are a poet, and if you can describe it well, it proves that you are a good poet; but that is very far from proving that you are a believer. Perhaps you can also weep in describing faith, that would then prove that you are a good actor'. (FSE 42–3)

Kierkegaard's position is clear – faith is not a matter of assent to doctrines, it is not a matter of belonging to a particular religious group and taking part in their rituals. Faith is shown in how one's life is lived – those alone have faith who trust their whole life to God, for whom God is at the centre of everything that they do and think and for whom the whole of life is viewed as lived *coram Deo* (before God or 'in the heart of God', as Luther puts it). Others may talk about faith and lecture about faith – but they do not have it. Faith may therefore be found in the very simple persons whose whole lives rest on God. They will know themselves to be sinners and failures but they accept that God loves them not because they are good or virtuous. God loves them as they are – warts and all. This is the hardest thing of all for the strong, independent individual to understand (Kant certainly could not accept it) but it is what faith involves. Anything else is an exercise in self-deceit.

7

Ethics and the relationship to God

Ethics, authority and religious duty

In previous chapters we have seen that for Kierkegaard, Christianity is based on the claim that Jesus is fully God and fully human, a claim which goes against reason. He regarded this claim as a paradox which can only be assented to once reason is relegated to second place – it demands a faith response which rejects the primacy of philosophy and rationality. This faith response, however, is not a matter of intellectual assent but of an existential commitment – a commitment to stake one's whole life on something that cannot be proved to be true and, indeed, which goes against reason. It demands a commitment to live in a relationship with God and try to see one's whole life in terms of this relationship. Both the aesthetic and the ethical stages in life end, for Kierkegaard, in despair. It is only in the religious stage, when God is at the centre, that an individual's real identity and eternal destiny can be found.

This picture, however, raises an important issue, namely that if the ethical is not the highest stage then it is possible for a faith relationship with God to call an individual beyond the ethical. Kierkegaard discusses this in *Fear and Trembling* (whose pseudonymous author is Johannes de Silentio), a detailed analysis of the biblical story of Abraham and Isaac.

It is not altogether clear what Kierkegaard means by 'ethics' in this context. In Kierkegaard's Denmark, the philosophy of Hegel was dominant, although the influence of Immanuel Kant was still strong. According to Kant,

> even though something is represented as being commanded by God . . . yet, if it flatly contradicts morality, it cannot, despite all appearances, be of God (for instance were a father ordered to

kill his son . . .). (*Religion within the Limits of Reason Alone*, tr. Greene and Hudson, 81)

For Hegel, morality is that which is for the good of society as a whole – ethics is concerned with the good of all human beings and this good is found in society and in community. Indeed, Kierkegaard quotes Hegel as going so far as to say that to have the limited outlook of a single individual is 'a moral form of evil' and to remain in this state is to be in 'sin or in a state of temptation . . .' (FT 83). For Hegel, then, one's highest duty is to society and to other human beings within society. The British Hegelian philosopher F. H. Bradley provided an early example of this approach. Bradley rejected all ethical absolutes and maintained that human beings were educated into moral duties and obligations. He put the position cogently in a chapter of his book *Ethical Studies* entitled 'My Station and its Duties'. Bradley maintains that a person

> is what he is because he is a born and educated social being, and a member of an individual social organism; that if you make an abstraction of all this, this is the same in him and in others, what you have left is not an Englishman, nor a man, but some I know not what residuum.

In other words, apart from the community that forms us, we are nothing. There is no inner nature, no individuality other than that coming from our shared background, and such individuality as we have comes from differences in formative influences. Thus the child

> is born not into a desert, but into a living world, a whole which has a true individuality of its own . . . And I fear that the 'individuality' (the particularness) which the child brought into the light with him now stands but a poor chance, and that there is no help for him until he is old enough to become a 'philosopher' . . . he is not for one moment left alone, but continually tampered with . . . the tender care that tends and guides him is impressing on him habits, habits, alas, not particular to himself, and the icy chains of universal custom are hardening themselves round his cradled life. . . . Is he now to try to develop his 'individuality', his self which is not the same as other selves? Where is it? What is it? Where can he find it? . . . In respect of education, the one true answer is that which a Pythagorean gave to

him who asked what was the best education for his son. 'If you make him a citizen of a people with good institutions.'

Kierkegaard rejects this position: it is one of the central marks of his whole approach to philosophy, theology and psychology that the individual before God is primary and conformity to society and its obligations are secondary. Some, of course, will argue that there is no tension between duty to society and, through society, to ethical principles and duty to God. Duty to God, they would hold, is the same as ethical duty and if one is obeying ethical commands then one is also obeying the commands of God. This approach is found among many religious people, including Orthodox Jews, who would see duty to God expressed as obedience to Torah – the commands of God laid down in the first five books of the Hebrew scriptures, which are seen as written by Moses. This approach is also seen in Islam, where obedience to God is fulfilled in obedience to the Holy Qur'an. A related approach can be found in Catholicism, where reason can work out, using natural law, what actions should be performed to guarantee human fulfilment. All these approaches see ethics and duty to God as coterminous. There is, perhaps, a difference between the approach taken by Orthodox Jews and Muslims on the one hand and Catholic Christians on the other, as the first two will see ethics as based on God's commands whereas Catholicism, following St Thomas Aquinas, will see God as having created human beings with a common human nature and the Bible as confirming an ethical approach to life which can also be arrived at by reason. Kant and Hegel go further down this path and regard ethics as entirely a matter of reason, with no need for revelation. However, where all these approaches agree is that duty to God and duty to ethics are the same. Kierkegaard disagrees.

If duty to God is no more than duty to ethics, then, Kierkegaard maintains, all that is happening is that ethical duty is being given a new name. Essentially, on this view, there is no such thing as a direct duty of the individual to God and one's duty is entirely expressed in ethics, which is mediated by the texts supposedly dictated or inspired by God, by the Church or religious community, or by those in authority.

Authority is vital in most religions and Kierkegaard questions where this authority stems from. For text-based religions such as

Orthodox Judaism and Islam, authority stems from the text which is provided by God. In Catholicism, it stems from the teaching authority of the Church. Thus the Catholic Church teaches that certain actions are morally wrong, on the basis of rational analysis and also revelation, and this teaching is then meant to be binding on all faithful Catholics. For instance, the Catholic Church teaches that the use of artificial contraception such as condoms or the pill is morally unacceptable. *In vitro* fertilization is rejected and so is embryonic stem-cell research. Once the Church's Magisterium (its teaching authority) has decided on a particular ethical position, this is authoritative for the faithful Catholic. The Catholic document *Veritatis Splendor* refers explicitly to 'authoritative teaching' by the 'Successors of Peter' (¶ 3) and says:

> The faithful are obliged to acknowledge and respect the specific moral precepts declared and taught in the name of God, Creator and Lord. (¶ 76)

and again:

> the Church's Magisterium also teaches the faithful specific particular precepts and requires that they consider them in conscience as morally binding. (¶ 110)

Germain Grisez, one of the foremost Catholic moral theologians, says:

> We believe that our Lord teaches in and through the Church and gives us the word of the Father. Hence, our submission to the Church's teaching is not submission to mere human opinions, but to the very word of God. (*Christian Moral Principles*, 570)

It is not, however, quite as simple as this.

A central question in Catholic ethics today is the role of conscience. Traditionally Catholicism after the Second Vatican Council (1962–5) has stood for the view that, over and above the teaching authority of the Church, individual conscience reigns supreme. In recent years, however, the Church has moved away from this position to maintain that it is not permissible to appeal to individual conscience in defence of acting against the teaching authority of the Church (hence the claim in *Veritatis Splendor*, quoted above, that the teaching of the Magisterium is morally binding).

Grisez claims that a faithful Catholic is not in a position to think that any moral doctrine proposed by the Pope or the Magisterium is wrong unless he or she can appeal to either scripture or to previous teachings of the Magisterium, and even these limited exceptions hardly apply to papal teaching:

> In the case of Papal teaching, however, there is little chance of its being undercut by a superior theological source. (*Christian Moral Principles*, 849)

Grisez maintains that even if one is wrong in following Church teaching, one is not responsible for being wrong, since following Church teaching is equivalent to following one's conscience. Individual conscience on this view needs to be informed or guided by the teaching of the Church and cannot go against it.

Kierkegaard rejects this, as this is to give priority to an institution or a set of ethical rules over the individual's direct relationship with God. Since, as we have seen, Kierkegaard insists on the love-relationship with God as being central, he refuses to accept that this relationship can be mediated or supplanted by an institution or any set of ethical rules. In saying this, of course, Kierkegaard makes clear his Protestant background – he is a Lutheran and sees direct obedience to God as being central.

These issues are brought clearly into focus by the story of Abraham and Isaac.

The faith of Abraham

In the book of Genesis, God commands Abraham to sacrifice his son Isaac, even though God has previously promised Abraham that through Isaac he would have innumerable descendants. Genesis records God's command as follows:

> God tested Abraham, and said to him . . . 'Take your son, your only son Isaac, whom you love, and go to the land of Moriah, and offer him there as a burnt offering upon one of the mountains of which I shall tell you.' (Genesis 22.1–2)

Some modern biblical commentators hold that the Abraham and Isaac story is fictitious – the story was inserted as a prohibition against child sacrifice and was never seen as a test of Abraham's faith. Kierkegaard never took this position – for him, the story is pivotal in Judaism in showing the faith of Abraham. It is also a central story in Christianity, where Abraham is described as the father of faith (see e.g. Galatians 3.7) – it cannot easily be dismissed. What Kierkegaard refuses to do is accept a superficial analysis or reading of the story. He sets out to explore its implications in some detail. Kierkegaard sees Abraham as the paradigm of an individual who puts obedience to God in first place and everything else, including his ethical obligations, in second place.

Abraham's whole life was one of obedience to God. Muslims see Abraham as the first person to submit to Allah, the first to give total obedience to one God. The Holy Qur'an records that Abraham preached worship of a single God in his home town and was persecuted because of this. Abraham destroyed the idols in the temple and was forced to flee. The Hebrew scriptures record that Abraham left his homeland in obedience to the command of God, and he remained faithful to God through many trials. He believed God's promises to him – that he would have a son and that through this son he would have innumerable descendants. He continued to believe in this promise long after it ceased to make rational sense. Even when Abraham's wife Sarah was past the menopause he still believed that God would give them a child. He trusted God in every aspect of his life. Three angels came to visit Abraham (in Christian Orthodox theology this is seen as a visit by the Holy Trinity) and they said that Sarah would have a child – and Sarah, who was inside Abraham's tent and who overheard the prophecy, laughed. The angels asked her why she was laughing and she denied it – it is because of Sarah's laughter at the angels' prophecy that the son is called Isaac, which means laughter.

The angels also revealed secrets to Abraham; they said that the town of Sodom was to be destroyed because of the great wickedness there. Abraham argued with God, saying that God is Lord of the world and does justice – so how could it be just to destroy Sodom if there were fifty just men in the town? The angels agreed that if there were fifty just men the town would not be destroyed. Abraham went on to bargain with God, eventually managing to reduce the number of just men necessary for the town to be saved to ten – however, there are not ten just men in the town and it is destroyed.

When, eventually, Isaac was born, it was the greatest joy of Abraham's life. Isaac was his hope for the future and the culmination of his dreams. In the culture of Abraham's time there was no idea of life after death. An individual lived on through his children and Isaac was, therefore, the guarantee of Abraham's name being carried forward. His death without issue would be the greatest possible tragedy.

The highest ethical obligation that a father can have is to his child, and Isaac was the son of Abraham's old age, loved by Abraham above everything in the world, the child of promise for whom Abraham had waited his whole life. Then God called Abraham to sacrifice Isaac. God was asking the unreasonable, the irrational; after all, it was God himself who had promised that, through Isaac, Abraham would have innumerable descendants. How, then, could God command the killing of Isaac? By every ethical or rational understanding God's command was unacceptable – and Abraham would have been justified in ignoring the command or convincing himself that he was deluded. But Abraham did not do this.

Kierkegaard analyses various options that were open to Abraham. He could have obeyed God's command but inwardly given up on the promise God had made. Abraham did not do this. He could have obeyed the command but pretended that this did not come from God and that it was his own will that caused him to slay Isaac, thereby possibly saving Isaac's faith in God. Abraham did not do this.

Abraham's response was to trust God and to do what God commanded – even though he could not understand. Abraham set out to sacrifice Isaac but – and this is vital – at the same time he continued to believe in God's promise that through Isaac he would have innumerable descendants. The philosopher will, of course, say that this does not make sense; if Isaac is killed, then Isaac cannot be the source of innumerable descendants. Abraham's faith, however, went beyond what could be justified by reason: he trusted God even though he could not make sense of his faith. He trusted that he would be 'the father of many nations' and that this would be fulfilled through his only son by his wife, Sarah: 'through Isaac shall your descendants be named' (Genesis 21.12).

Abraham has grounds for his faith and his response is not as absurd as Kierkegaard would have it appear. Abraham's obedience to God was not an isolated instance; his whole life had been based on love for and trust in God. He had left Ur on God's instruction, he had parted from Lot on God's command and his wife had conceived long after the menopause because of God's intervention. Abraham's grounds for faith in God were considerable. Nevertheless, Kierkegaard's point is that Abraham behaves against ethical rules and Kierkegaard's real concern is not to discuss an old story but to examine the relevance this story has for today and, particularly, the claim that a faith relationship with God may call an individual beyond the normal frontiers of ethics.

The knight of faith

In the previous chapter reference was made to what Kierkegaard terms 'the knight of infinite resignation'. This is the person who gives up the security of the ethical and, on the strength of his or her own will, relinquishes all those things that the temporal world finds important in order to seek God. Beyond this, however, lies another category – 'the knight of faith'. This is the person who is willing not only to resign the temporal world's priorities but also to trust in God and to have faith.

Either Abraham was a true 'knight of faith' – *or* he was deluded. The person who says that the ethical stage is the highest must maintain the latter, while Kierkegaard maintains the former. Essentially Kierkegaard is saying that it is possible for a command from God to call the individual beyond ethics. Normally, the temptation to act outside an ethical framework originates in personal desire and, if anyone gives in to such temptation, then he or she is guilty of moral failure or, in theological terms, he or she sins. Society will condemn such an individual, insisting on repentance and conformity to the ethical. As we have already seen, the ethical stage may be demanding, but essentially it is 'safe' – everyone can understand and admire ethical behaviour and everyone will be quick to condemn and disapprove of those who infringe ethical norms. Kierkegaard's question is whether it is possible for a person to be called to act outside an ethical framework and *not* be in sin or error. In other words, are the categories of sin and ethical failure coterminous? Is sin always equivalent to acting unethically? Kierkegaard's answer to this is no.

If the religious stage is a possibility, then an individual may be called outside the frontiers of normal ethics by their relationship with God. Kierkegaard's point is that this is a conceptual possibility and, if this is the case, then it may be a temptation to continue to abide by the 'safe' demands of ethics. In other words, if God calls you to act in a certain way and if reason, convention, the demands of the community or an individual's own sense of what is 'appropriate' proclaim this as 'wrong' or 'mistaken', then to give in to these demands is itself a temptation. To take an example, St Francis publicly repudiated his father outside Assisi cathedral. He had an ethical duty of obedience to his father but he rejected this in favour of what he considered to be a higher calling from God.

Following the command from God, Abraham is portrayed as setting out for Mount Moriah. His love for Isaac remains unchanged; what he sets out to do is undertaken solely in obedience to God:

> The absolute duty can then lead to what ethics would forbid, but it can by no means make the knight of faith have done with loving. (FT 101)

As he sets out his love for his son is unchanged and he does not tell anyone what he is about to do. He does not tell his wife, or his servants, or his son – how could he? They would all have regarded him as mad and tried to stop him. Silence is forced on the person who enters the religious stage and here again there is a contrast with Hegelian ethics:

> The Hegelian philosophy assumes there is no justified concealment ... it is therefore consistent in its requirement of disclosure. (FT 109)

The ethical rejects the idea of secrecy whereas both the aesthetic and the religious require secrecy and silence; but the aesthetic and the religious are essentially different despite that one similarity. Abraham *cannot* speak because nothing he can say will make him understood (FT 137). Abraham is the paradigm of the person for whom language no longer serves as a means of communication. Unlike the Tragic Hero who is called on by ethics to sacrifice one ethical duty for another (see Chapter 5), Abraham has no higher ethical objective; he does not act to benefit his community or his family and from the outside it may seem that he is driven by his own selfish desires. He is in absolute isolation. People can understand and admire the Tragic Hero – but who, Kierkegaard asks, can understand or admire

Abraham? He is called to put into second place that which he loves most in the world, his son. Not only that, but Abraham is called to act against reason. God has, after all, promised Abraham that, through Isaac, he will have innumerable descendants – yet God commands Abraham to kill Isaac. This does not make sense: it can only appear to Abraham as if God is denying his original promise. Abraham, however, has faith: he trusts God even though he cannot understand and Abraham regards his duty to God as the highest duty.

Kierkegaard's pseudonymous author Johannes Climacus asks why Abraham acts against ethics. His answer is clear: 'For God's sake, and what is exactly the same, for his own' (FT 88).

The teleological suspension of the ethical

Kierkegaard believes that there can be such a thing as the teleological suspension of the ethical. In other words, ethics may be relegated to second place because an individual has a higher *telos* or end – namely a relationship with God. A duty to God, therefore, can call someone beyond the frontiers of ethics in response to a command from God. If this is not the case, then Abraham is mad or deluded. Only if there is the possibility of an absolute duty to God is it possible to make sense of Abraham's action in setting out to sacrifice Isaac.

In today's world it is important to recognize the dangers involved in the claim that a duty to God can call someone beyond the frontiers of what is ethically acceptable. Many mad, deluded, deceived or deranged individuals do this:

- In 1994, Paul Hill, a former Presbyterian minister, murdered an abortion doctor, John Britton, and his bodyguard James Barrett in Florida. He made no attempt to avoid arrest, employed no lawyers and called no witnesses during his trial, claiming throughout that his actions were justified by a command from God to protect the innocent and exact justice on a mass murderer. Before he was executed in 2003, he said, 'I can honestly say, if I had not acted when I did, in the way I did, that I could not look myself in the mirror'. He claimed to look forward to death because he 'knew' that God would be pleased with him.
- In the September 11 attacks on the World Trade Center in New York, those who carried out the attacks were convinced that they

were acting in direct obedience to God. Suicide bombers who kill civilians and others often do so because they are convinced that this is what God requires of them and, if they do this, they will be rewarded by being taken straight to Paradise.

• When Peter Sutcliffe, the so-called 'Yorkshire Ripper', was arrested in 1981 his defence for having brutally murdered 13 women was that he was acting as a 'tool of God'.

Kierkegaard, therefore, seems to be advocating a view that opens the possibility for people to claim 'obedience to God' as a way of justifying morally reprehensible actions that any reasonable, ethical person would deplore. There is a sense in which this is indeed the case – although it is not quite as simple as this.

Once the security of the ethical is abandoned then the individual faces a real danger – is he or she in fact being obedient to God or is he or she mad, deluded or simply deceived? It would be easy to argue that Abraham was simply deluded when God supposedly asked him to sacrifice Isaac. Kierkegaard is open to this possibility although he recognizes that if one makes this claim then ethics is supreme. Since Judaism, Islam and Christianity all give a pivotal role to Abraham, effectively a central part of the main monotheistic tradition would be undermined. Kant, as we have seen, would endorse precisely this view, as any possibility of acting against ethics and rationality leads to all the dangers that madness and delusion bring with them.

One mark of sanity may be an ability to ask oneself whether or not one is mad; there is, perhaps, a difference between the 'knight of faith' acting in 'fear and trembling' and the steely certainty of Paul Hill or Peter Sutcliffe. When asked 'What if you were mistaken?', Paul Hill responded, 'If I'm wrong, I don't imagine that that could be the case' (<http://news.bbc.co.uk/1/hi/programmes/newsnight/3080708.stm>). Kierkegaard fully recognized the danger of delusion and accepts that there is no easy way to determine who is the person of faith and who is the fanatic. Those in the ethical stage will condemn them both because of their secrecy and will insist that both conform their wills to its dictates. Again this emphasizes the loneliness of the path taken by the person who really tries to live in a subjective relationship with God – there is no security, no certainty, no objective test. The individual is alone, dependent on faith and with the knowledge that it is always at least possible that he or she could be mistaken. This is a position of extreme vulnerability. It would be far safer and more secure to abandon this relationship to God and instead to conform to the demands of the Church or other community in which one lives. After all, these can be widely understood and the person who lives in the ethical sphere will be respected and admired. The religious stage involves the individual being alone before God with no guarantee of any security – except the security that comes from the relationship with God itself. Further, all religious figures have recognized what St John of the Cross refers to as 'the dark night of the soul' – there are times when God seems to be absent and prayer seems to be empty – and to stake one's life on a relationship with God when God does not seem to be there is a tall order.

An important point to recognize is that Abraham is called to make a sacrifice – the word is important and is often ignored today. To sacrifice something means giving up something one does not want to give up. In this case, it meant Abraham being willing to sacrifice his most precious and beloved son and to put loyalty to God first. In a sense this is what Abraham's test was finally about – it was a question whether or not Abraham would put duty to God above all other considerations. Throughout his life Abraham had been tested and the command to sacrifice Isaac was the ultimate test. In the case of the September 11 bombers they were not sacrificing anything except their own lives. They were killing people who were innocent but with whom they had no connection at all. There is very little element of sacrifice in doing this.

The single most important sin in the Hebrew scriptures is fornication – but this is not understood sexually. It means to put something other than God at the centre of life. The first commandment is very clear – it calls individuals to put the love of God at the centre of their lives. Nothing must get in the way of this. There must be no idols, no greater loves. It is this that was being tested in the story of Abraham and Isaac – whether, in the final analysis, Abraham would sacrifice even his most cherished love for his son if called to do so by God. Suicide bombers are not in this position.

Kierkegaard is careful to separate the demands of the Church as recognized and accepted by society (which he terms 'Christendom') and the demands of God. Too often, he maintains, the demands of God are abandoned by priests and Church leaders, who instead substitute demands that are comfortable and simply involve conformity to accepted standards of behaviour. The scandal of the gospel is done away with and the offence of the Absolute Paradox is eliminated.

The key issues

There are two separate issues here.

(1) Is it possible for a duty to God to override one's duty to ethics? Kierkegaard deals with this in Problema II (FT 96ff.), a section which is entitled 'Is there an absolute duty to God?' He concludes this section as follows:

> either there is an absolute duty to God, and if so then it is the paradox that the single individual as the particular is higher than the universal and as the particular stands in an absolute relation to the absolute – or else faith has never existed because it has existed always; or else Abraham is done for. (FT 108)

In other words, if there is no such thing as an absolute duty to God which can override ethical duty, then 'faith' is merely compliance with ethics and has no distinctive role.

(2) How does one know that what one considers to be a call from God is genuine and not a delusion? Kierkegaard rejects any easy answer to his question and maintains that it is always possible to be mistaken.

The difficulty of determining (2) does not, however, rule out (1) as a live possibility and Kierkegaard clearly maintains that a duty to God can override ethical norms. Abraham, of course, is a paradigm; Kierkegaard believes that knights of faith exist in every age. They will not be immediately visible, however. They are concealed and will look exactly like ordinary men and women; no external sign may be detectable, because the essential quality of the knight of faith is interior. No outsider can claim that someone else is or is not a knight of faith; the simple as much as the clever person may be a knight of faith. Faith, for Kierkegaard, is the great equalizer – the one thing that every human being can have in common no matter what the background or circumstances.

Silence and an absence of words are essential to Kierkegaard's understanding of a life lived in relationship with God – yet he himself is aware of a tension here, as he expends great effort and many words in trying to help people to understand what the faith relationship requires. He is using words to force people into silence and a consideration of self. Communication with others usually involves blunting the challenge imposed by living with God. As Kierkegaard says: 'Silence in the relationship to God is invigorating... talking about one's God-relationship is an emptying that weakens' (J 3988). This is why he stresses indirect communication. People have to be brought to see something whose reality cannot be grasped by words.

It is significant that in the area of a direct, individual relationship with God, in the possibility of secrecy and acting against Church teaching, Kierkegaard differs markedly from Augustine, Thomas Aquinas and other theologians. Richard Price, in his book *Augustine* (London: HarperCollins, 1996), quotes his subject as saying: 'Each person is to think the same about his soul. Let each man hate to have a feeling he cannot share with others' (82).

Kierkegaard maintains that a call from God may enforce silence on an individual and may call such a person outside both ethical and generally accepted Christian norms. Augustine sees Christianity as essentially a communal affair, both in the Church on earth and with the saints in heaven. Kierkegaard emphasizes the individual journey of faith and the priority of the individual in relation to God. Kierkegaard does not reject community, but he does believe that genuine community can only be found amidst people who have first become individuals. This, for Kierkegaard, is the real aim of a Christian community – to strengthen each other on the individual journey to God while recognizing that everyone is a failure and yet is loved unconditionally by God. For Kierkegaard, it is the experience of this love and its acceptance that is crucial. This love is transformative – it makes the person into a new individual who will then be enabled to show this love and understanding to everyone else.

8

The truth of the God-relationship

Purity of heart

Kierkegaard did not believe that there were any outward signs of whether someone was or was not genuinely living in a God-relation-ship. The relationship was subjective and could not be measured in objective terms. Yet one of Kierkegaard's concerns was to hold a mirror before his reader and enable them to decide whether he or she is in a genuine God-relationship. *Purity of Heart is to Will One Thing* is Kierkegaard's great spiritual classic. It is particularly significant because it is written under his own name and also specifically dedicated to 'that solitary individual', the highest cate-gory of existence, which Kierkegaard had previously outlined. A 'solitary individual' is somebody living life before God, and it is to this state that Kierkegaard himself aspired. The book is based on James 4.8: 'Draw near to God and he will draw near to you. Cleanse your hands, you sinners; and purify your hearts, you double-minded' (see PH 53).

Purity of heart is stated to be a 'Spiritual Preparation for the office of Confession'. Kierkegaard never specifically states that 'the one thing' which he calls his reader to will is the God-relationship, but this is clear from the text and from other books, for instance:

> Now the question is, Wilt thou be offended or wilt thou believe? If thou wilt believe, then thou must pass through the possibil-ity of offence, accept Christianity on any terms . . . So, a fig for the understanding! So you say, 'Whether it now is a help or a torment, I will one thing only. I will belong to Christ, I will be a Christian. (TC 117)

For Kierkegaard, this is the essential test for someone who wishes to be a Christian – whether she or he will, with passion and total inner conviction, stake everything on the desire to belong to Christ, to live in relationship with God and to place God at the centre of the whole of life.

'If there is something eternal in a man,' says Kierkegaard, 'it must be able to exist and to be grasped within every change' (PH 36). The individual's relationship to the Eternal does not depend on any outer factors: neither youth nor age, poverty or wealth, sickness or health, worldly success or failure. The individual should never outgrow the Eternal and only the Eternal is always relevant and is always present no matter what the outer circumstances. The presence of the Eternal

> is like the murmuring of a brook. If you go buried in your own thoughts, if you are busy, then you do not notice it at all in passing. You are not aware that this murmuring exists. But if you stand still, then you discover it. And if you have discovered it, then you must stand still. And when you stand still, then it persuades you. And when it has persuaded you, then you must stoop and listen to it attentively. And when you have stooped to listen to it, then it captures you. (PH 49)

In prayer, God does not get to know something, but the person praying gets to know something about him- or herself. Prayer does not change God, it changes the person uttering it. Kierkegaard maintains that in prayer we learn something and the refusal to learn about ourselves is the greatest possible loss:

> there is an ignorance that no one need be troubled by, if he was deprived either of the opportunity or the capacity to learn. But there is an ignorance about one's own life that is equally tragic for the learned and the simple, for both are bound by the same responsibility. This ignorance is called self-deceit . . . The ignorant man can gradually acquire wisdom and knowledge, but the self-deluded one if he won 'the one thing needful' would have won purity of heart. (PH 52)

For Kierkegaard, then, purity of heart involves 'knowing yourself' but, unlike the god Apollo, whose catch-phrase this was, for Kierkegaard it means knowing oneself before God:

> Purity of Heart is the very wisdom that is acquired through prayer. A man of prayer does not pore over learned books for he is the

wise man 'whose eyes are opened' – when he kneels down. (PH 55)

For Kierkegaard, repentance and remorse for sin are both important – they are guides to deepening the individual's understanding of self in relation to God and must not be passed over quickly. An individual needs to reflect on his or her failings and on what changes to self are needed – the individual must be self-conscious or conscious of self. Precipitate repentance is false (PH 44), and one needs to reflect on one's failings in order to understand better the sort of person one is in contrast to the sort of person one needs to become. This is not a matter of guilt but of reorientation. Hence a time of preparation for confession is important. One's failings in fact reflect a failure to will sufficiently passionately the 'one thing' that Kierkegaard considers to be paramount. Sin is not a question of acting immorally; it is a much deeper concept which entails a failure of passion or love in relation to God.

Willing one thing

To 'will one thing' is to will to be 'that solitary individual' and to live your life wholly in relationship to God. This is the only focus or centre for life which can be singular and not 'double-minded' – having a variety of motives. All temporal objectives, whether they be power, money, reputation, security, marriage, children or happiness, are multiple and cannot stay constant in every single situation in life. There are many temptations which call the individual away from willing one thing – including the temptation to aim for what is impressive instead of the relationship with God. In particular, there are barriers that get in the way of this single-minded concentration on living in relationship with God, and Kierkegaard identifies these as follows.

Willing the good out of a hope of a reward

Someone who succumbs to the 'reward-disease' may start out willing to live in a relationship with God and may, with enthusiasm, continue for a time. However, he then faces opposition and although at first he never desired to be rewarded in this world, he finds the effort too difficult to keep up. Gradually, therefore, he lets go of his concentration on God and instead seeks approval from others: he cannot stand their opposition or the loneliness that comes from willing one thing single-mindedly, so he ends up relating himself to the temporal world and forgetting the Eternal. This, Kierkegaard contends, is a common state of affairs – a person sets out on the journey of faith wanting nothing more than a relationship with God but this proves too hard and lonely a path, so instead the person seeks to be recognized and rewarded by the community of which he or she is a part. It is no longer, then, the relationship with God that is primary.

Willing the good out of fear of punishment

The fear of punishment Kierkegaard has in mind here could be fear of punishment from other human beings, or of punishment from God. For Kierkegaard, the fear of God is the beginning of wisdom. People often talk of the love of God and ridicule anyone who actually lives his or her life in fear and respect for God. As he puts it,

> spiritually understood there is a ruinous illness, namely, not to fear what a man should fear; the sacredness of modesty, God in the heavens, the command of duty, the voice of conscience, the accountability of eternity. (PH 80)

The fear of God is not the same as fear of punishment. Duty to God is, for Kierkegaard, an absolute – a categorical duty undertaken for itself alone and not for any other reason. Fear of punishment is something else. A person who fears punishment

> does not will the Good, he wills it only out of fear of punishment. Therefore – if there were no punishment! In that 'if' lurks double-mindedness. If there were no punishment! In that 'if' hisses double-mindedness. (PH 83)

Such people are only seeking God out of fear (whether it be fear of other people or of eternal punishment) and if the fear of punishment was removed they would no longer seek God. Underneath their desire for God is their desire to be free from the pain that punishment would cause; their lives are focused not on a single God-relationship, on 'one thing', but on both the desire for God and the desire for personal comfort. Such people are double-minded. Fear is

> a dry nurse for the child; it has no milk; a blood-less corrector for the youth; it has no beckoning Encouragement; a niggardly

disease for the adult; it has no blessing; a horror for the aged. (PH 85)

It is not possible to develop a love-relationship with God in which the primary motive is fear. To claim that this is possible is to be double-minded. Love seeks no reward and has no motive. Kierkegaard holds that the world has no power over an individual who is truly trying to 'will one thing'.

> To be sure the world has power. It can lay many a burden upon the innocent one. It can make his life sour and laborious for him. It can rob him of his life. But it cannot punish an innocent one. How wonderful, here is a limit, a limit that is invisible . . . When the good man stands on the other side of the boundary line inside the fortification of eternity, he is strong, stronger than the whole world. (PH 97–8)

This strength is based on a love-relationship which is not driven by any motive other than the relationship itself. Like Kant, Kierkegaard believed that the highest good is the will which loves the Good for its own sake.

The egocentric service of the good

This barrier to willing one thing is erected when the person who supposedly wills that the Good should triumph in the world actually wants to ensure that the triumph should be through him. He is essentially self-centred and feeds on the feeling of pride that his success engenders:

> When a man is active early and late 'For the sake of the Good', storming about noisily and restlessly, hurling himself into time, as a sick man throws off his clothes, scornful of the world's reward; when such a man makes a place among men, then the masses think what he himself imagines, that he is inspired . . . he wishes to sacrifice all, he fears nothing, only he will not sacrifice himself in daily self-forgetfulness. This he fears to do. (PH 101, 103)

Kierkegaard claims that God does not need human beings and the conceit that God does need a particular individual for God's purposes to succeed is, in fact, merely human pride at work. The idea that one is 'needed' by God is, essentially, egocentricity, and this is the *real* motive for the individual's action. Such a person is not being single-minded in trying to relate to God; he or she is subconsciously feeding their ego, and may indeed be a deluded inhabitant of the aesthetic stage.

Willing the good to a certain degree

'At bottom,' Kierkegaard says, commitment to a certain degree 'is the way all double-mindedness expresses itself' (PH 106). In trade or commerce or in any other aspect of life, people compromise all the time – the pressure of work and other commitments increase and God is relegated to a minor role. As Kierkegaard says:

> this press of busyness is like a charm. And it is sad to see how its power swells, how it reaches out seeking always to lay hold on ever-younger victims so that childhood or youth are scarcely allowed the quiet and the retirement in which the Eternal may unfold a divine growth . . . It is true that a mirror has the quality of enabling a man to see his image in it, but for this he must stand still. If he rushes hastily by he sees nothing. (PH 107–8)

If the individual would really achieve purity of heart and really wishes to relate him- or herself wholly to God and to live this relationship out, then 'busyness' and activity can be the biggest temptation. It is so easy to think that what one is doing is 'important' or that it 'matters', but where God is concerned this may be an excuse for the individual to concentrate attention on him- or herself and his or her own recognition by the world and not on patient, humble service to God. In *Walden* Thoreau wrote,

> When we consider what . . . is the chief end of man, and what are the true necessaries and means of life, it appears as if men had deliberately chosen the common mode of living because they preferred it to any other. Yet they honestly think there is no choice left. (ch. 1a, 'Economy')

One thing soon leads to another and eventually it becomes almost impossible to change. We are all occupied; how easy would it be to stop, apparently do nothing, while reorienting oneself to God? Kierkegaard considers this exceptionally hard – but being hard is not the same as being impossible.

The role of suffering

Kierkegaard believes that anyone who seriously tries to remain loyal to God and puts the temporal world in second place will *necessarily* suffer. Jesus' call, 'take up your cross and follow me', is inescapable. First, the crowd will try hard to get such a person to conform to their will, to water down his or her commitment and to compromise. If he or she submits to what is expected, then popularity and success may well result – but the Eternal will have been abandoned. It is worth noting clearly here that by suffering Kierkegaard does not mean the suffering of illness, disappointment, hurt, etc. to which all human beings are prone. He is referring to two other things. First is the suffering that will necessarily come to anyone who tries to follow Jesus and who puts God in the centre of one's life. Just as Jesus was despised and rejected by the crowd, so will any who follow him. Second, however, is the pain of actually trying to become a self, to become what a human being is capable of becoming when this is so different from what human nature will choose if left to its own devices.

Kierkegaard admits that some will say that such suffering is 'useless' and does not 'achieve' anything, but this is to look at things from a temporal rather than an eternal perspective. To measure what is worthwhile in terms of results is precisely to objectify religion and to deny its essentially subjective nature. An individual may be alone and abandoned by others because he or she is trying to follow God, but God will never abandon him or her. It is at this point that 'cleverness' comes in; but it is generally a cleverness which convinces the individual that he or she is mistaken, that God does not really want this suffering, that it is better to compromise, to 'achieve' something and to harmonize with the world. This is temptation, albeit a subtle and clever form of temptation.

Kierkegaard's message here is uncompromising and, it must be admitted, out of tune with what many regard as the Christian message. Not many today emphasize suffering, yet for Kierkegaard it is an essential result of discipleship:

This is the test: to become and remain a Christian, through sufferings with which no other human sufferings can compare in painfulness and anguish. Yet it is not Christianity that is cruel, nor is it Christ. No, Christ in Himself is gentleness and love . . .

the cruelty consists in the fact that the Christian has to live in this world and express in the environment of this world what it is to be a Christian . . . the more the Christian is inwardly in fear and trembling before God, so much the more is he in dread of every false step, so much the more is he inclined only to accuse himself. In this situation it might sometimes be a comfort to him if others thought well of him. But exactly the opposite is the case . . . the more he labours in fear and trembling, struggling all the time to be more entirely unselfish, devoted and loving, all the more do men accuse him of self-love. (TC 194–5)

Christianity, according to Kierkegaard, requires the individual to live out life focused on God and not on the temporal:

Christianity is still the only explanation of existence which holds water. The earthly existence is suffering; every man has his share, and therefore his dying words are: God be praised, it is done with. This earthly existence is the time of test, is the examination . . . You and I are being examined our whole life long. (J 1052)

God chooses and is closest to the despised, the cast-offs of the race, one single, sorry, abandoned wretch, a dreg of humanity. (J 4231)

To love God and to be happy and fortunate in this world are not possible. (J 2443)

The one thing that unites every single man and woman in the world, of no matter what race, age or financial circumstance, is the ability to be a single individual relating directly to God. This eliminates all temporal distinctions and makes every human being equal to every other. The only goal in life that can endure through all contingency, through all alterations of circumstances, is the goal of single-mindedly willing to be in relationship with God. If one does this and lives the whole of one's life accordingly, then one will not be afraid of eternity's judgement. All human beings will, after death, have to account for their lives and the accounting will not be in terms of what they have achieved, how much money they have made or how popular they are – no, the accounting will be based on the extent to which they have lived in relationship with God and allowed this relationship to guide every facet of their lives.

The complete absence of any guarantee of a reward for a life of faith makes Kierkegaard's Christianity difficult to accept. Even Kant, who could not countenance doing good and living in relation to what he saw as universal truth out of hope for reward, had to point to the satisfaction gained from the certainty of being right and the possible benefits of creating a better society in order to make sense of his demand for people to do right. Kierkegaard could not even accept these forms of reward – for him there can be no certainty in the relationship with God and little hope that the struggle of individuals could ever make much of a difference to society in general. Nevertheless if an individual's whole life is based on trust in the love of God, this will provide a peace and a reassurance that can be found nowhere else.

In the previous chapter we saw that Kierkegaard insisted that truth is to be found in the individual's subjectivity, but that this was not a relativistic claim. The objective truth of Christianity (if, of course, it is true and Kierkegaard accepted that this could not be proved) had to be lived out in a day-by-day relationship to God. Determining whether one is in this relationship is a matter for each individual and, essentially, involves 'willing one thing' and purity of heart. More needs to be said, however, as to how an individual can *discern* whether or not he or she is in a relationship with God. Part of this involves the avoidance of self-deceit by seeking to uncover the real motivations for one's actions as outlined in this chapter – but it will also necessarily involve a consideration of what an individual means by love. Kierkegaard's understanding of Christian love is radical and this will be examined in the next chapter.

9

Works of love

Faith and works

We have seen that, for Kierkegaard, coming to Christianity involves
making a choice between offence at the paradox of the God-man
or faith. Faith requires reason to be set aside and for the individual
to depend wholly on God, putting God at the centre of all concerns.
However, it would be easy to caricature such a position and to maintain that it is essentially pietistic, requiring only individual faith with
no commitment to action in the world – indeed such a charge is fre-
quently levelled at Kierkegaard. However, this is to misunderstand him.

Kierkegaard maintains that both faith and works are required for
the Christian. The debate between Luther and the Catholic Church
is sometimes crudely caricatured as a debate between the primacy of
faith and the primacy of works – but Kierkegaard shows that it is not
as simple as this:

> in every human being there is an inclination either to want to
> be meritorious when it comes to works or, when faith and grace
> are to be emphasized, also to want to be free of works as far
> as possible. Indeed, 'man', this rational creation of God, certainly
> does not let himself be fooled; he is not a peasant coming to
> market, he has his eyes open. 'No, it's one or the other,' says man.
> 'If it is to be works – fine, but then I must also ask for the
> legitimate yield I have coming from my works, so that they are
> meritorious. If it is to be grace – fine, but then I must also ask
> to be free from works – otherwise it surely is not grace. If it
> is to be works and nevertheless grace, this is indeed foolish-
> ness.' Yes, this is indeed foolishness; that would also be true
> Lutheranism; that would indeed be Christianity. Christianity's

requirement is this: your life should express works as strenuously as possible; then one thing more is required – that you humble yourself and confess: But my being saved is nevertheless grace. The error of the Middle Ages, meritoriousness, was abhorred. But when one scrutinizes the matter more deeply, it is easy to see that people had perhaps an even greater notion that works are meritorious than did the Middle Ages, but they applied grace in such a way that they freed themselves from works. (FSE 16–17)

So works are required, but the individual will not see any merit in the works in making him- or herself *really* 'deserve' salvation; nothing that human beings can do can atone for their essential sinfulness and they can be saved only by grace. Similarly, in terms of a faith response to God, the individual must venture and strive to develop the relationship, but nevertheless hold steadfastly that faith is a free gift from God. Faith depends entirely on God having become man in order to bridge the gap between the human and the divine. To anyone saying that faith must either be striven for or a gift, that the two poles cannot be brought together and that there is an either/or here, Kierkegaard would say that faith is indeed foolishness – the foolishness that makes Christianity folly to the Greeks and the philosophers.

What, then, does Christianity require from the person who has faith? At one level Kierkegaard would consider this an inappropriate question. If one is seeking a list of objective criteria against which one could measure whether someone was living a Christian life, then Kierkegaard would maintain that this was to misunderstand the issue radically. As we have seen, faith is essentially subjective and there is no clear outward manifestation of it – not even the virtuous or ethical life, since this is not the same as a life lived in relationship with God. The life of faith essentially involves willing one thing – placing God at the centre of everything one does.

However, Kierkegaard is quite specific that a life lived in this way will necessarily involve love. Possibly his most significant book is one that is seldom read and has until recently been out of print for some years in English. This book is entitled *Works of Love*, first published in 1847.

The role of love

Kierkegaard maintains that most love is preferential and therefore selfish. Love of a partner, of children or of friends is not Christian love. Indeed these are types of preferential love which Kierkegaard considered to be positively dangerous, as they tend to encourage an exclusive, inward-looking love of a small group which is opposed to the non-preferential love which Christianity requires. The duty to love one's neighbour is commanded by Christianity and it is a direct consequence of faith. Jesus says 'Thou shalt love . . .' Love is not an optional extra, it is a command to love everyone, irrespective of race, colour or creed. It is a command to love irrespective of appearance, irrespective of all temporal or worldly differences. 'Love makes no distinctions – and we must love everyone equally rather than seek to make everyone equal' (WL 70).

The task of Christians is not to strive for social equality so that everyone is equal in a worldly sense, but rather to recognize that everyone is equal irrespective of worldly differences. Kierkegaard sees the fundamental equality of all human beings as an equality before God and once this is truly recognized then everyone must be loved equally as children of God. This love is not merely theoretical, it must be a passionate and committed love which is costly and demanding.

Kierkegaard does not reject married love or friendship; still less does he reject the power of the erotic and of sexuality. However, he does believe that these loves must not be put into first place – *all* loves, even the love involved in marriage and children, must be secondary to the centrality of the relationship with God. As Kierkegaard says:

> Your wife shall first and foremost be your neighbour; the fact that she is your wife is just a narrower definition of your special relationship to her. (WL 141)

In any relationship, God must be the middle term – each relationship should be a triangle involving two people with God in the middle:

> Love cannot be just between people – that would merely be Eros or friendship. Christian love must be between three for God is always the middle term. (WL 46)

As soon as God is eliminated, all loves become selfish. True love of neighbour does not depend on being loved in return – it is unconditional.

'However much the beloved changes, the Lover never varies in his love – Love abides' (WL 281). This applies to God's love of human beings, which remains unchanged no matter what we do. God's love is not earned, it is not a reward for virtue. God loves human beings as they are and seeks to woo them to be more like God. Similarly human beings should love unconditionally – which is why forgiveness should come easily to Christians, who are really trying to follow Christ, as love does not hold grudges and is always ready to think the best of another.

Kierkegaard does not reject self-love – indeed he emphasizes that Jesus called his followers to love others *as themselves*. In order really to love ourselves Kierkegaard argues that we must live in relationship with God and develop to be real individuals. Similarly if we really love others we must seek to bring them to the same position:

The Christian view means this: Truly to love oneself is to love God; truly to love another person is with every sacrifice (even to become hated) to help the other person love God as well. (WL 119)

As John Saxbee pointed out in a paper given at the annual Kierkegaard dinner in the Danish Church in London on the anniversary of Kierkegaard's death on 11 November 1990, Kierkegaard identifies everyone as our neighbour in the global village to which we belong and he redirects our attention away from the outward and visible 'what' of giving and loving to the 'how' of Christian love. Saxbee quoted Kierkegaard:

'If that man famous through eighteen hundred years, the merciful Samaritan, if he had come walking, not riding, on the way from Jericho to Jerusalem where he saw the unfortunate man lying, if he had brought nothing with him whereby he could bind up his wounds, if he had then lifted up the unfortunate man and placed him on his shoulders, carrying him to the nearest inn where the keeper would take in neither him nor the unfortunate one because the Samaritan did not have a penny, if he could only beg and beseech the hard-hearted innkeeper nevertheless to be merciful because it involved a man's life – if therefore he had not . . . but no, the tale is not yet done – consequently, if the Samaritan, far from losing patience over this, had gone away carrying the unfortunate man, had sought a softer resting place for the wounded man, had sat by his side, had done everything in his power to halt the loss of blood – but the unfortunate man died in his arms; would he not have been just as merciful, equally as merciful as that merciful Samaritan, or is there some objection to be lodged against calling this the story of the good Samaritan?' (WL 294)

Saxbee says that there is, indeed, no objection to be lodged here and Kierkegaard 'scores a palpable hit'. Everyone can love irrespective of their circumstances just as everyone is to be loved, not because they are inherently lovable, but because God commands it. When we pick out some favoured ones to love or when we love those whom we like, this is not Christian love. Kierkegaard has a parable which draws a parallel with two artists. One artist toured the world looking for someone beautiful to paint and never found anyone adequate to his skill. The other artist stayed at home and found something beautiful to paint in every person he encountered. Which, Kierkegaard asks, is the true artist? Just as with the artists, so it should be with the Christian. People should love others not because they deserve to be loved or because they have lovable features but because all women and men are lovable. If we cannot see this, the fault is in us rather than in the others.

Kierkegaard has a point here which seems right intuitively, but it must be questioned whether all people can be loved in this way. Is it practical to love the SS guard if one is a Jewish prisoner who has just had her baby's brains splattered across a wall? Ettie Hillesum asked herself this question as she waited with other prisoners in a camp in Holland to be transported to one of the death camps. She looked at the faces of the guards, trying to find something loveable there, and found it exceptionally hard. Is it possible for a woman in wartorn Bosnia or Rwanda to love the men who are serially raping her? These challenges are trenchant but, if they are valid, they should be directed against Christianity itself and not simply against Kierkegaard. Kierkegaard is surely expressing one of Christ's fundamental commands. Whether this command can be lived out in practice is another issue.

10

Inter-religious dialogue

Kierkegaard wrote in Denmark in the middle of the nineteenth century. Denmark was almost entirely Lutheran; there were hardly any Muslims, Hindus, Sikhs, Buddhists or members of other religions present and the small Jewish community of Copenhagen seems to have had little impact on his writing. It would be very easy, therefore, to hold that Kierkegaard has nothing to offer to the contemporary debate about inter-religious dialogue – yet this is far from the case. His approach to religion has a major contribution to make, albeit one that most scholars have not been aware of or developed.

There is one particular passage in *Concluding Unscientific Post-script* that is relevant, but whose application Kierkegaard did not develop as much as he might have done. His task was to reintroduce Christianity into Christendom – to wake up a society that considered itself to be Christian but which, he felt, fell far short of such an ideal. He did not consider a world in which many different religions competed against each other or how one would balance the competing truth-claims of different religions. As we have seen, Kierkegaard believed in a realist understanding of truth-claims about religion – either God exists or God does not, either Jesus was God incarnate or he was not. There was no way of proving these statements and, indeed, they went beyond reason. The incarnation was the Absolute Paradox, requiring reason to be suspended and faith to accept something that philosophy or reason could not understand. If God exists and became human in the person of Jesus, then God did this out of love and the possible responses are either to reject this claim entirely (which Kierkegaard considered perfectly rational) or to accept it. Acceptance did not mean mere intellectual assent to a creedal formula, however. It meant staking one's life on these claims and seeking to live out a relationship with God, which places God at the centre of the individual's life and requires all temporal interests, concerns and relationships to be given second place.

Given the stress that Kierkegaard places on the truth-claim of the incarnation, it would seem that he might be described as a Christian exclusivist. This would mean that he considered that Christianity was the only road to truth and to personal salvation and that every other religion was false and to be rejected. However, this would be to misunderstand his whole work.

While affirming the objective truth of Christianity, Kierkegaard also argued that being a Christian did not consist in being baptized, participating in church services or sacraments, or even agreeing to creedal formulations. Christianity was about a love-relationship with God which placed that at the centre of an individual's life. Is it, then, possible that this love-relationship might be arrived at from a non-Christian background? Kierkegaard is quite clear that faith is not a matter of assent to doctrinal formulations – it is a relationship. A relationship is judged by the quality of the relationship. As noted earlier, *Purity of Heart* is written under Kierkegaard's own name and is dedicated to 'that solitary individual' – that person to whom, above all others, Kierkegaard is seeking to communicate. It asks individuals to examine themselves, to strip away self-deceit and to see whether they really are centring their lives on God, the Unknown (as Kierkegaard often refers to God) or whatever is ultimate. There are many forms of self-deceit by which individuals can convince themselves that they are really trying to relate to God when in fact they are not. But the 'pure in heart' are those who, honestly and truthfully, centre their whole being on a love-relationship with God. Kierkegaard is clear that this relationship can be entered into by someone who may have an incorrect theology and a totally in-valid conception of God. The passage from *Concluding Unscientific Postscript* that makes this most clear is the following:

> If one who lives in the midst of Christendom goes up to the house of God, the house of the true God, with the true conception of God in his knowledge, and prays, but prays in a false spirit; and one who lives in an idolatrous community prays with the entire passion of the infinite, although his eyes rest on the image of an idol, where is there more truth? The one prays in truth to

God though he worships an idol; the other prays falsely to the true God and hence worships in fact an idol. (CUP 180)

The key phrase is 'The one prays in truth to God though he worships an idol' – it is the quality of the relationship that is determinative. If the individual is in a relationship with God then it is God to whom he or she is related, whatever the name being used. The same point is made in C. S. Lewis's book *The Last Battle*, in which the story is told of a young officer in the Calormenes, Emeth, who has fought against the people of Narnia. He has served his god Tash and has been brought up to hate the name of Aslan, the great lion who represents Jesus. Emeth appears before Aslan after the Calormenes lose the battle. The scene then unfolds as follows:

But the Glorious One [Aslan] bent down his golden head and touched my forehead with his tongue and said, 'Son, thou art welcome.'

But I said, 'Alas, Lord, I am no son of thine but the servant of Tash.'

He answered, 'Child, all the service thou hast done to Tash, I account as service done to me.'

Then, by reason of my great desire for wisdom and understanding, I overcame my fear and questioned the Glorious One and said, 'Lord, is it then true, as the Ape said, that thou and Tash are one?'

The Lion growled so that the earth shook (but his wrath was not against me) and said, 'It is false. Not because he and I are one, but because we are opposites, I take to me the services which thou hast done to him. For he and I are of such different kinds that no service which is vile can be done to me, and none which is not vile can be done to him. Therefore if any man swear by Tash and keep his oath for the oath's sake, it is by me that he has truly sworn, though he know it not, and it is I who reward him. And if any man do of cruelty in my name, then, though he says the name Aslan, it is Tash whom he serves and by Tash his deed is accepted. Dost thou understand, child?'

I said, 'Lord, thou knowest how much I understand.' But I said also (for the truth constrained me), 'Yet I have been seeking Tash all my days.'

'Beloved,' said the Glorious One, unless thy desire had been for me thou wouldst not have sought so long and so truly. For all find what they truly seek.' (ch. 15)

The point is clear – the Calormene officer's belief was false but he lived in such a way that he was actually in a relationship with Aslan even though he was not aware of it. Iris Murdoch, in *Metaphysics as a Guide to Morals*, discusses the nature of truth in religious belief. She also concludes that it is the sincerity of the God-relationship that determines the validity of the 'God' that is worshipped. She tells the parable of a village that believes it is in possession of a holy relic; everybody venerates it, centres their lives around it and, in the end, because of their faith the dog's tooth (for that is what it is) glows with light because it is sincerely venerated. The devout Muslim who submits whole-heartedly to Allah, the Jew who centres his or her life wholly on God, or the committed and focused Hindu, Sikh or Buddhist may be closer to God because of the life they have lived (in other words, because of their subjectivity and the passion of their relationship) than the person who may have more correct objective facts about God but who does not translate this into a life of faith – where faith involves a subjective relationship with God.

Many books have illustrated this and, interestingly, Jesus makes the same point. When he was asked what will happen on the last day, when the sheep and goats are separated, he does not reply that those who worship correctly or who have the correct theology will be accepted. Rather the division will be between those who have cared for the sick, those in prison, those who are hungry and in need, and those who have not (Matthew 25.31–46). The former may be atheists but will be closer to God than the latter, who may be 'good Christians' but who, Kierkegaard would say, were just going through the outward appearance of being Christian without any of the subjective commitment that is required. The writer of the epistle of James makes this same point:

> But be doers of the word, and not hearers only, deceiving your-selves. For if anyone is a hearer of the word and not a doer, he is like a man observing his natural face in a mirror; for he observes himself, goes away, and immediately forgets what kind of man he was. But he who looks into the perfect law of liberty and continues in it, and is not a forgetful hearer but a

doer of the work, this one will be blessed in what he does. If anyone among you thinks he is religious, and does not bridle his tongue but deceives his own heart, this one's religion is useless. Pure and undefiled religion before God and the Father is this: to visit orphans and widows in their trouble, and to keep oneself unspotted from the world. (James 1.22–27)

Interestingly, Luther did not accept this epistle as authoritative; it seemed to undermine the Pauline idea that Christians are justified or saved by their faith. Lutheran Christianity built on the principle that baptism and adherence to Christian creeds was the route to salvation and became exclusivist. Kierkegaard could be seen to be redressing the balance – accepting the priority of faith, but reminding his reader that a faith which is limited to words means nothing.

Kierkegaard's perspective on faith can open up a new way of understanding inter-religious dialogue. Instead of focusing on discussions about belief systems and what is true or false, the real dialogue that is needed is between those who are trying to live the life of holiness no matter what their creed. These people will exhibit lives of gentleness, compassion and goodness and, in spite of different cultures, these qualities shine through. Nelson Mandela, Martin Luther King, Gandhi, Vaclav Havel, Guru Nanak, the Buddha, the Hindu sages, Zoroaster, Plato and Aristotle show a quality in their lives which does not depend on a particular belief system. Kierkegaard recognizes this. This is not to make truth-claims relative but to say that it is the way we live that matters – those who seek the Absolute, the Ground of our Being, Ultimate Reality, Allah, Yahweh, God, Jesus or the Undifferentiated Unity, and seek to live life obedient to the absolute demand made on them, may be closer to each other than the millions who pay lip service to religion but for whom it is not a lived reality. Kierkegaard says, 'As you have lived, so have you believed'. It is our lives that express our beliefs – not our words – and if there is to be an accounting, we will be accountable for the lives we have led.

11

Kierkegaard and the Church

St Augustine spent his life as a bishop defending the Church from heresies such as those of the Manichaeans, the Arians, the Pelagians and the Donatists. For Augustine, salvation lay through membership of the Church – not all those within the Church might be saved, but outside the Church there was no salvation. The Roman Catholic Church, even though some of its members were reluctant to deny worthy Protestants a part in the church of Christ, continued to adopt this position up until the declaration of the Second Vatican Council, *Lumen Gentium* (1965), which deals with the salvation of non-believers. Most great Christian thinkers, while at times being critical, have nevertheless been loyal members of the Church and have spoken against it mildly and gently, if at all. Kierkegaard was far more ambiguous in his view – in fact he was often downright critical of the Church. For most of his life he attended the Lutheran Church of Denmark regularly and preached at times. He considered ordination at various stages of his life but never took the final step – partly because he felt a call to be a writer and partly because his frustration with the Church was possibly too great. He ended his life with one of the most devastating attacks on the Church ever written. These attacks were made in a series of articles which have been collected together in a book entitled *Attack upon Christendom*. The articles were published between 1854 and 1859.

The occasion for the attack was the funeral oration following the death of Jakob Mynster. Kierkegaard had known the old bishop well for much of his life and when Professor Haus Martensen delivered an address calling Mynster a 'witness for the truth', Kierkegaard's patience snapped. For Kierkegaard, a 'witness to the truth' was a quite specific term – it ranked with the apostles as the highest of Christian categories. Mynster's virtue, in Kierkegaard's eyes, was that he had fully recognized that he did not belong in this category at all. Kierkegaard saw Martensen's funeral oration as a cynical exercise in drawing attention to the orator, namely Martensen himself, who was seeking the bishopric made vacant by Mynster's death. Kierkegaard withheld his attack until Martensen was appointed and then let forth his protest.

The protest started with an attack on Martensen but it soon widened to an attack on the whole Church, on priests and on the social institution which the Church had become. Kierkegaard maintained that many priests and churches no longer proclaimed the Christian gospel; instead they proclaimed a message of comfort and good cheer. They sought a comfortable living for themselves and the Church provided them with security, respectability and a position in society. Kierkegaard did not think that Christianity was comfortable. Priests and churches were 'making a fool out of God' by proclaiming something that was utterly alien to the Christianity of the New Testament (AC 59).

Some commentators have said that Kierkegaard's criticism of the Church was a late development, but this is not the case. His negative views on the clergy and 'Christendom' (which identified the Church with the nation) are present throughout his writings. One of his publications, *Judge for Yourselves!*, asks his reader to visit any church on a Sunday and to judge for themselves whether what is there proclaimed is the same as the Christianity of the New Testament, which involved passion, commitment and total dedication:

> 'Christendom' is not the Church of Christ . . . Not by any means. No, I say that 'Christendom' is twaddle which has clung to Christianity like a cobweb to a fruit, and now is so polite as to want to be mistaken for Christianity . . . The sort of existence which the millions of 'Christendom' give evidence of has absolutely no relation to the New Testament. (AC 192)

The role of the New Testament

Kierkegaard, therefore, is not rejecting the true church of Christ, made up of the fellowship of those who are sincerely and passionately trying to follow Christ in humble obedience. What he is rejecting is the institutional church, which is a travesty of the real thing.

The same point is applied to the New Testament, which Kierkegaard sees the Church as sanitizing and diluting. As one of his parables says:

The New Testament . . . regarded as a guide for Christians [can] . . . become pretty much like a guidebook to a particular country when everything in that country has been totally changed. Such a guidebook serves no longer the serious purpose of being useful to travellers in that country, but at the most it is worth reading for amusement. When one is making the journey easily by railways, one reads in the guidebook 'Here is Woolf's Gullet where one plunges 70,000 fathoms down under the earth'; while one sits and smokes one's cigar in the snug café, one reads in the guidebook 'here a band of robbers has its stronghold from which it issues to assault the travellers and maltreat them', here it is, etc. Here it is; that is, here it *was*; for now (it is very amusing to imagine how it was), now there is no Woolf's Gullet but the railway, and no robber band but a snug café. (AC 111)

Kierkegaard does not reject 'the guidebook', which is the New Testament; indeed he is affirming its continuing relevance and importance to life today. What it is to be a human being and the journey each person has to make are essentially the same as when the New Testament was written – but so often this is not recognized and the Bible becomes a historical curiosity. Kierkegaard rejects those who dismiss the relevance of the Bible as much as he rejects the safety and security of those in the train (the Church) who no longer feel themselves individually accountable to it. We can see here the influence of the Reformation idea of an 'open Bible', giving all believers direct access to the word of God. For Kierkegaard, although he was aware of current developments in biblical scholarship, the Bible nevertheless represented a clear handbook which could guide someone who wished to live a life accountable to God. Kierkegaard also criticized those biblical scholars who spend their time in critical examination of the Bible rather than being radically accountable to it. He asks his reader to imagine that a king issues a royal command to all of his subjects, but instead of that command being obeyed, it becomes the object of analysis and a huge literature about its style and origins. Instead of 'true seriousness' representing radical accountability to the Bible, biblical scholars busy themselves with textual exegesis (FSE 58–9).

Dean Bloch, in an article published in April 1855, threatened Kierkegaard with 'ecclesiastical sanction' because of his attacks. Kierkegaard's response was characteristic:

> If I do not reform, the Dean would have me punished ecclesiastically. And how? Indeed the punishment is cruelly devised; it is so cruel that I counsel the women to have their smelling salts at hand in order not to faint when they hear it. If I do not reform, the church door will be closed to me. Horrible! So then, if I do not reform, I shall be shut out, excluded from hearing, on Sundays during the quiet hours, the eloquence of the witnesses to the truth. (AC 47)

Kierkegaard's sarcasm is obvious – the Bible is still available to him and he is still accountable to and loved by God. The 'true worship of God consists quite simply in doing God's will' and the Church is not absolutely necessary for this (AC 219). Soon Kierkegaard came to feel that he could not in conscience continue to 'make a fool of God' by taking part in Sunday worship. Salvation does not depend on the dictates of priests – but upon God. The priests make a good living and acquire respect and admiration by talking in lofty terms on Sundays, but what they talk about is intended to bring comfort to their flock and security to themselves – they do not talk about Christ's message because it is too challenging and uncomfortable.

In a parable (J 3067), Kierkegaard likened the Church to a building into which farmyard geese went each Sunday. An elder goose preached and talked about the love of the great Goose in the sky and how he had made geese with wings so that they could fly. Every time the great Goose's name was mentioned all the geese bowed – and so it went on every Sunday. They came and went into the building but their life was otherwise the same. One goose, however, was foolish enough to take the story seriously and instead of being concerned with life in the farmyard he spent his time trying to fly and to use the wings he had been given. Everyone said how foolish he was, yet finally he took to the air, flew around and came back and told everyone that the stories were true and that the other geese also could use their wings – but they ignored him. And so life went on, until

Christmas, when all the geese were cooked for Christmas dinner except the one who had learnt to use his wings.

Ibsen, in his play *Brand*, develops a similar image. The eponymous main character, a priest, returns to settle in the remote village of his childhood, seeing it as his duty to bring Christianity to the people there. He sacrifices his ambition, and eventually his wife and child, in pursuing that duty. He decides to build a church; he believes that its physical presence will bring the people in and change their lives. Yet he becomes so obsessed with the church building that he alienates the people who should fill it, the real 'church', and is driven out of the community. Up on the wintry mountainside Brand has a terrible moment of realization. He has built his life on a misinterpretation of what faith requires. At the beginning of the play Brand meets a childhood friend and his new fiancée walking beyond the village. He calls out to them, warning them that they are on an ice-bridge and risking their lives in walking together without due care for the reality around them. At the end of the play the irony is that it is Brand who has always been on an ideological ice-bridge, risking all on his faith in God. He had sought to live his whole life in obedience to God but at the end of his life he feels that he has misunderstood what God really requires. He has invested his life in a church building rather than in people. The play ends with an avalanche – a very literal representation of Brand's ice-bridge collapsing and pitching him into nothingness, albeit accompanied by a ringing voice proclaiming 'God is love'. Ibsen leaves us with an ambiguous picture of Brand staking his whole life on a relationship with God, coming at the end to recognize he has made major mistakes and yet, somehow, the love of God is still there for him.

Kierkegaard demands all or nothing – the 'knight of faith' may well lose everything and be driven out of his or her community but that is the price a real commitment to the God-relationship demands. *Either* God exists *or* God does not. However, if God does exist then it means the individual staking his or her whole life on the relationship with God and, even if mistakes are made, nothing can separate the individual from the love of God. For Kierkegaard, nobody can hedge their bets on God; lives cannot be staked 'either way'. As Pascal observed, the way we live will find us out – saying that you have faith but living an easy life boils down to having no faith. A positive decision must be made and must become the centre of one's life – but there can be no certainty that it is the right one. After all, if there was certainty no faith would be required.

Kierkegaard rejected much that was comfortable and normally accepted. As we have seen, he thought that marriage brought real dangers of a loss of individuality; that ceremonies such as baptism and confirmation were mere outward symbols while what Christianity sought was an inner, subjective transformation. He thought that the task of Christians must be to love others as they love themselves by helping to draw others to making a decision to become involved with God, and that membership of a church was not sufficient to make someone a Christian. He considered the incarnation to be a paradox, an offence to reason, and that anyone becoming involved with Christ would inevitably suffer as a result.

Christianity and social action

One of Denmark's greatest social reformers, Nikolaí Grundtvig, lived at the same time as Kierkegaard. Grundtvig has had an enormous influence on Danish education and Danish social policy – in almost every town in Denmark a Grundtvig high school or library is to be found. Kierkegaard, however, said that 'Grundtvig can never properly be said to have fought for Christianity; he really only fought for something earthly' (AC 185). The community and social policy were not Kierkegaard's concern and he would have thought that the concern of the Church with these matters today tends to minimize the importance of the individual and the individual's accountability to God. Social change comes not from a transformation of society but from a transformation of individuals – and becoming an individual is the most difficult task of all, which church membership can sometimes prevent as social convention within the Church is substituted for passion and real Christian commitment.

Kierkegaard and the Church

Kierkegaard certainly did not argue for the abolition of the church of Christ – far from it. What he warned against was the danger of mistaking the institution of the Church for Christ's Church. He saw his task as being to 'reintroduce Christianity in Christendom' (AC 28). He thought it would be easier in a missionary situation to bring

Christianity to people who had never heard of it than to bring people to see what Christianity involved when they already thought they were Christians. This was his difficulty – and all his writing involves trying to get people to sit up and take notice. He expected his books to be largely ignored or to be dissected by academics – but his task was to seek 'his reader', who would read quietly and would either allow the whole of life to be changed by accepting the challenge that Christianity really represents, or else reject it. Better, he would say, to be offended and to reject Christianity than to take part in the travesty of Christianity which the Church has so often become.

In the final months of his life, Kierkegaard would deliberately sit outside church on Sunday instead of joining in the worship – although he insisted on continuing to pay tithes of his income to the Church just in case anyone thought he would derive financial advantage from not attending.

He died less than six months after his final and strongest attack on the institutional Danish Lutheran Church, having collapsed in the street. He died giving thanks to God for having educated him on what it was to be a Christian. He refused to take communion from a paid servant of the state – in other words a priest who was paid by the Danish government, as all priests were at the time. Throughout his life, he saw God's hand guiding him – although this guidance was seen in retrospect and not at the time. He looked forward to heaven, where he would have nothing else to do but to give thanks. Since his death, Kierkegaard has had a huge influence on many seminal figures, including Ibsen, Miguel de Unamuno, Karl Barth, Kafka, W. H. Auden, C. S. Lewis, Gabriel Marcel, R. S. Thomas and many others – however, there is no space here to discuss these influences.

The fact that this book has not considered Kierkegaard's motivations and his psychological state is therefore a deliberate policy. If Kierkegaard's writing succeeds in its aim then such analysis is beside the point – perhaps he may be held to have succeeded despite the obstacles in his path, perhaps he succeeded because of these obstacles. The important point is whether he succeeds or not, not why he succeeds or fails. If he fails in his objectives, then analysis of his background may provide reasons to explain or excuse his failure and these may be interesting, but it is only an analysis of failure.

This book has not set out to argue for or against Kierkegaard's enterprise – rather, it is concerned to make clear what his enterprise was so that you, the reader, can be motivated to read further and then decide for yourself whether or not he succeeds. Hopefully, such an approach is entirely faithful to Kierkegaard's own intention.

Further reading

The brief sketch of Kierkegaard's life in Chapter 1 is due to many sources, but in particular to Walter Lowrie's *A Short Life of Kierkegaard* (2nd edn Princeton, NY: Princeton University Press, 1965), which, although somewhat dated and now out of print, is still the best resource. The Princeton editions of *Philosophical Fragments* and *Concluding Unscientific Postscript* also have relevant details.

Key books by Kierkegaard

Attack upon Christendom, tr. Walter Lowrie.

The Concept of Anxiety: A Simple Psychologically Orienting Deliberation on the Dogmatic Issue of Hereditary Sin, tr. Reidar Thompte.

The Concept of Irony, with Continual Reference to Socrates/Notes of Schelling's Berlin Lectures, Howard V. Hong and Edna H. Hong.

Concluding Unscientific Postscript to Philosophical Fragments, tr. Howard V. Hong and Edna H. Hong.

Fear and Trembling: Dialectical Lyric by Johannes De Silentio, tr. Alastair Hannay.

Fear and Trembling/Repetition, tr. Edna H. Hong and Howard V. Hong.

Philosophical Fragments, or a Fragment of Philosophy/Johannes Climacus, or De omnibus dubitandum est, tr. Edna H. Hong and Howard V. Hong.

Point of View on my Life as an Author, tr. Howard V. Hong and Edna H. Hong.

Purity of Heart is to Will One Thing, tr. Douglas V. Steere.

The Sickness Unto Death: A Christian Psychological Exposition of Edification and Awakening by Anti-Climacus, tr. Alastair Hannay.

Books about Kierkegaard

Gardiner, Patrick, *Kierkegaard: A Very Short Introduction* (Oxford: Oxford University Press, 2002).

Hannay, Alistair and Marino, Gordon D. (eds), *The Cambridge Companion to Kierkegaard* (Cambridge: Cambridge University Press, 1998).

Howard V. Hong and Edna H. Hong (eds), *The Essential Kierkegaard* (Princeton, NY: Princeton University Press, 2000).

Lippitt, John, *The Routledge Philosophy Guidebook to Kierkegaard and 'Fear and Trembling'* (London: Routledge, 2003).

Rée, Jonathan and Chamberlain, Jane (eds), *Kierkegaard: A Critical Reader* (Oxford: Blackwell, 1998).

Index